Contents

Figures

Tables

PART I

UK costs and benefits of EU membership

1. Introduction, the UK's relationship to the EU, the aim of this book and policy conclusions

The central theme of this book is that the European Union has developed economic policies in trade and regulation that do not conform to the liberal model of free markets under the rule of law. Instead they are protectionist and interventionist because of the pressures of political preferences and vested interests. The European Union Treaties proclaim with great clarity that the EU is a political project whose ultimate aim is complete political union and whose journey is guided by the process of 'ever-closer union'. While UK politicians have from time to time thought that it was a project for a single market moving towards full competition internally and full free trade internationally, this has not turned out to be correct. Instead the EU has introduced extensive social regulation, has attempted to integrate legal processes across borders, has intervened heavily in fiscal decisions of euro-zone governments, has pursued aggressive policies on climate change without attention to cost effectiveness, and has done much else – overall going well beyond and often in contradiction to that free market programme.

As part of these efforts the EU has worked untiringly to create political allies in all EU states within their business, personal and regional structures – in no country more so than the UK. Thus the business beneficiaries of EU protectionism are vocal in their support of the EU, whether in agriculture, manufacturing or services (such as the City). Regions in receipt of EU subsidies are in favour of the EU because of this perceived largesse, even though they involve a usual cost to the UK Treasury equal to 87 per cent of the EU payout since the 'UK rebate' falls by 67 per cent and matching funds of 20 per cent are typically required. At a personal level households receive regular information on how the EU has improved their tourism opportunities, their environment and their general interchange with other European peoples; they are told frequently by pro-EU politicians how they would face uncertainties and loss of jobs outside the EU. As a result the main organs of opinion favour staying in the EU, and the main business groups, regional lobbies and citizen interest groups

3

also lobby for this. It is thus easy to argue that the case for staying in is a 'business' one even though a moment's reflection reminds us that business opinion is not the same thing as the economic interests of UK citizens.

The viewpoint of this book is that of the economist. The book reviews the costs and benefits to UK citizens of the EU, much as the Manchester liberals Cobden and Bright reviewed the costs and benefits of the Corn Laws in the early nineteenth century; then too a large and powerful business (agricultural) lobby opposed repeal.

This book focuses mainly on the role of trade, the central function of the EU; while this is not we think the major source of costs to the UK, it has been widely misunderstood as an advantage of EU membership because it gives us 'access' to the EU market and to markets with which the EU negotiates trade agreements. This is a fallacy: the book is principally devoted to explaining that this is the case because international trade is about the price at which you can sell your exports and buy your imports. We then go on to explain how the EU is a customs union devoted to raising the prices at which we can buy imports and selectively raising the prices of our exports and that this protectionist strategy, like virtually all such strategies, reduces our welfare.

Because there are so many other facets of EU membership we also devote space to these. We consider regulation to be an obvious source of intrusion that many have seen is costly. With the euro-zone bringing about a surge in new controls from Brussels and reminding us that 'ever-closer union' must imply that the UK eventually joins the euro, we have added some material on the effects of this. Since the euro-zone crisis it has become apparent that 'bail-out' is a central feature of the euro-zone and indeed of the EU, which has forced countries outside the euro such as ourselves to help out too; we have updated our review of the possibilities of the UK being involved in transfers to the rest of the EU in the future. A further topic that we have devoted some space to is immigration, now a central part of the UK political debate and closely linked to the free entry of people from the rest of the EU. Finally, much concern has been expressed about what the world trading environment would be like for a free trading UK outside the EU; we have added sections looking carefully at this. Other than these central issues, we have generally updated the factual background and the review of other work in this edition.

The book is organized into two main parts. The first is devoted to summarizing the economic issues involved in EU membership. Some of these are not to do with trade: regulation, the euro, possible bail-out demands, and of course the basic membership fees. Much has been written on these issues and we attempt to build on this and give our own summary account of costs and benefits, using models we have developed that give us some ability to calculate these. Then we consider trade and the ways in which our EU membership diverts us from free trade to our ultimate cost. Many, as pointed out above, believe that at least in this respect the EU is a fine institution, contributing to opening up trade barriers around the world. Thus some have argued we should leave the EU, 'except in trade'. But this is a quite wrong assessment and was originally the cause for writing this book. We devote the fourth chapter to determining a broad estimate of the costs the EU's wide protectionist agenda has imposed on UK (and indeed EU) citizens.

In the second part of the book we devote three full chapters to the full story of what the EU has done in the areas of trade in agriculture, manufacturing and services. These chapters set out in considerable detail both the facts and available analyses of how trade and trade protection has developed, especially in the EU, and how much this distorts trading patterns around the world.

The rest of this chapter is effectively both an introduction to the book and an extended 'executive summary' of it.

THE AIM OF 'BREXIT' – OR BETTER 'BRESET'

'Brexit', as it is popularly known, is therefore the topic of this book. But this conjures up pictures of bad-tempered 'departure' and 'divorce' followed by either a poor relationship with the EU or none at all. However, this is not what we believe to be the alternative to continuing in the current EU. Let us accept for a start that 'renegotiation' of the current EU Treaties (as summed up in the latest Lisbon Treaty) is not a realistic idea since the changes the UK would require would mean a rewriting of many treaty areas and these changes in turn would need unanimous agreement from all member states of the EU. While no one can prevent politicians from attempting such a renegotiation of the Lisbon Treaty, its prospect of success is vanishingly small. What we have in mind in this book is something else – a new treaty between the UK and the EU which for both sides would embed what is good and would eliminate the current sources of endless mutual discontent.

As we will see in detail in the following pages, the UK suffers from excessive direct intervention in UK economic and political affairs from the EU. Most of all, it suffers from the uncertainty of what 'ever-closer union' might bring in the way of additional interventions. In the costs we enumerate, the biggest potential costs lie ahead, in the form of possible measures implied by current EU aims. Thus 'opt-outs', such as that we have currently from joining the euro, cannot be considered safe in this longer-term perspective. We already saw how one such opt-out, from the Social Chapter, was ceded by the Blair Labour Government, no doubt as part of some imagined trade-off with benefits to be obtained from Brussels or merely as a way of ushering in 'socialism by the back door'. This event illustrates how easily the UK could be sucked into more and more EU intervention by remaining a member of the EU under the present treaty; whether it happens by EU pressure or by willing complicity on the part of UK politicians whose agenda of the moment it might suit (but who may later regret the cumulative effect of their actions), there is a ratchet effect at work in this EU relationship as defined in the Lisbon Treaty. That treaty never surrenders any powers the EU has acquired (the 'acquis communautaire') and hence any surrender from the UK side accumulates its losses of control; each time we surrender, our politicians say 'ah well, it is easier to give in and to stay in than to try to change the beast' and thus it is we find ourselves some forty years since entry into 'the Common Market' in an all-pervading 'European Union' relationship we never seriously dreamt of, let alone intended.

What is needed instead is a new bilateral treaty which defines a limited relationship, limited in its current and future scope to definite areas of mutual benefit – let us call it a 'resetting' of our relationship with the EU or 'Breset'. As we will see, this will include cooperation in trade and regulation, preserving the best of what we now have of these, while jettisoning the excessive protection and over-regulation (notably in the labour market) and the threats of their future extension which we abhor. Being 'out' of the EU will then imply a far more flexible relationship with the EU in which good shared regulation and trade relationships will be preserved. The fears expressed by many about being 'out' will be seen to be groundless in this perspective.

We will develop the details of this new relationship in what follows. But here we sketch the basic idea. At the core of our relationship with the rest of the EU lies the Single Market, which is intended to prevent country regulation from acting as a trade barrier, and free trade access throughout the EU's geographical area. Though this does not extend much to services, our key UK sector, it greatly affects our manufacturing industry. As we will see later, the problem with this lies in its high level of protectionism through the EU's Customs Union policies which keep out or restrict imports of non-EU products: it is not only in its well-known Common Agricultural Policy that the EU is protectionist. Somehow therefore we need to extricate ourselves as a major trading nation from the EU's protectionism while preserving the benefits of the Single Market and free trade within the EU. This can be done. In the first place, where the UK feels that product regulations are helpful to industrial integration, they can be left alone and protected in a new treaty. Secondly, where trade barriers are concerned, it is possible for the UK to maintain free bilateral trade with the EU, while also removing trade barriers against other countries, in industries where there is a high degree of integration between the UK and the rest of the EU. This is possible because the way that the EU mainly levies its protection is via trade agreements on access and pricing; so effectively in these highly integrated industries (such as the volume car industry) the UK would continue to price its products in the rest of the EU as it now does. Even though imported products from the rest of the world would drive UK prices down to world levels, these lower prices would not filter through into the rest of the EU.

The idea of a new UK–EU treaty would therefore be to preserve the existing relationships that achieve virtuous integration. But at the same time the UK would not implement regulations that damaged the economy as a whole. The idea that trade is held up by differences in regulation that have a distant relationship to the trading industry (such as general labour market regulations) is not accepted in WTO judgements or in the theory of trade; differences between countries' institutions are a valid source of cost differences, and contribute to competition. So UK regulations will in general be based on UK judgements of cost–benefit. Nor would the UK adhere to the single market in labour, rather exerting normal immigration controls based essentially on skill points, as in the US 'green card' system. It would withdraw *sine die* from any potential involvement in the euro or in trans-EU bail-out arrangements. It would agree to mutually advantageous extradition arrangements but not to any pooling of justice systems. It would cooperate with the EU foreign office just as it does with the US State Department. It would join forces with the EU in general talks on trade, such as the one currently going on with the US, where all sides stand to benefit from agreement.

In short the UK would once again become a sovereign country, friendly with its large neighbour just as it is friendly with countries such as the US, Canada and Australia, and it would agree to close trading and regulatory relationships with the EU as needed for mutual benefit. It is wrong to suggest that such a new treaty cannot be achieved because of the ill-will generated by our demands, though of course it is possible that negotiations for a new treaty would break down, at least for a time. In this book we do our costing on the basis of breakdown and we show that it is worth the UK's while to leave even on this basis; essentially leaving without any new UK–EU treaty would be to adopt a role as a free trading nation in the WTO community, with all our other existing political relationships such as NATO, the OECD and the IMF, and there is absolutely no problem about such a role, as we explain in detail below. But since there is mutual gain to be had, relative to breakdown, in both sides reaching a new treaty, it is illogical to suggest it will not be achieved – just as it has been achieved between the EU and both Norway and Switzerland. Once all sides realize that departure is going to happen anyway, all bluffing and threats will be removed and realism will produce discussions on a new treaty. Usually countries, like people, in the end do what is in their interests.

RECENT DEVELOPMENTS: THE EURO-ZONE CRISIS

The euro-zone crisis is likely to continue for a number of years, with the European Central Bank (ECB) acting as a backstop until agreement is reached on a new institutional structure sufficiently reassuring to Northern Europe that its transfers to Southern Europe will have a good chance of being repaid. The UK's exclusion from the euro has meant that it is neither vulnerable to the panic that has engulfed Southern sovereign bonds nor in direct line to make transfers to the crisis-stricken South.

The institutional framework now being developed implies a high degree of monitoring and intervention by creditor countries of debtor countries within the euro-zone. There will be controls on bank behaviour, targets for governments, and new financial taxes. While in principle this will take place within the euro-zone, there will be pressure to extend it to all EU countries on the grounds that other EU members could 'undercut' euro-zone arrangements. The UK will be seen as an offshore competitor with banks, businesses and governments that, being in the euro-zone, are burdened with these controls and regulations. Such competition will be argued to be unfair under the Single Market, for which Qualified Majority Voting applies. It would be easy to extend these things to the UK by majority vote.

Furthermore, the pressures for protection will increase in order to produce as much euro-zone growth as possible, for best prospects of debt repayment. Serious recessions for long periods such as the euro-zone has been undergoing make such pressures intense. The UK suffers at present from the degree of protection for the EU as a whole. This protection will probably increase; even within the EU covert protection against non-euro countries could occur.

At best, the euro-zone will be obsessed with the euro crisis for the coming decade, stalling any progress in liberalizing markets and in increasing competition, things that could have lessened the costs of membership to the UK. This tendency for the euro to strengthen the drive towards excessive regulation as a way of bolstering the single currency was something widely foreseen at the start of the euro. But the crisis is likely to make this much stronger.

Table 1.1   A survey of costs from EU membership

	(% of GDP)
Net UK contribution	0.5
Costs of Common Agricultural Policy and of EU protection of manufacturing	4.0
Regulations	6–25
Bail-out transfers	2–9
Effects of EU regulations on growth to 2035	0.5 p.a.
Effect of joining the euro on economic volatility	Doubling of volatility

Sources: See discussion in later chapters.

For the UK this prospect is extremely damaging. Even without any change in the status quo the economic costs to the UK of the EU are substantial: Table 1.1 summarizes the estimates we make in the rest of this book; we have reviewed our estimates in the first edition in the light of more up-to-date information since. The main change has been the rise of trade with China, which has led to a further wave of protectionism, at the same time as protectionism against older competitors such as South Korea has diminished. Meanwhile EU-inspired social intervention has continued to make inroads into UK life, the latest one being widespread rights for temporary workers. With the changes the euro crisis threatens, these costs have increased towards the upper end of the possible spectrum identified in the table. Recent work has also identified possible effects on growth, while we include also the effects of eventual joining of the euro on the economy's business cycle volatility.

A contrary and popular argument for the benefits of the EU to the UK revolves around Foreign Direct Investment (FDI). However, this argument is entirely fallacious. FDI brings benefits because of technological spill-overs from foreign firms, which raise productivity. The UK economy's productivity is likely to be maximized when comparative advantage is allowed its fullest rein, that is, outside the EU, under free trade. If this structure implies that industries operating in the UK are more efficient, then less FDI will be required. But this will reflect the fact that the UK is more productive, not less.

Another argument is that leaving the EU would imply costs of 1–3 per cent of GDP due to the imposition of the EU's Common Tariff on the UK (see Ottaviano et al., 2014). This is to be compared with our calculated gain of around 4 per cent of GDP.

As we noted above, we would in practice aim for a new treaty which would preserve the helpful aspects of our trade relationships, notably good common regulation and bilateral free trade. Thus the calculations of Ottaviano et al., which come up with a net loss of UK welfare from leaving the EU leave out two important elements:

> They do not factor in the effect of moving to free trade with the rest of the world (ROW) from existing EU protective measures. Since on our calculation the EU levies tariff-equivalents on the rest of the world of about 10 per cent, this omission would generate large negative effects if included in their calculation. They appear to assume that the UK would levy the same tariff-equivalents on the rest of the world (accounting for around half UK trade), whereas in our view the UK would move to free trade vis-à-vis all countries. Certainly that is the policy we propose on 'Brexit'/'Breset' and so it should be costed accurately.
>
> They assume that the EU would react by raising trade and regulative barriers against UK exporters even though we impose no such barriers on EU exporters to us; as discussed above, this is highly unlikely because EU industries are closely integrated in many cases with UK industry and the UK market. They would be damaged by difficulties in accessing UK input products and would fear retaliation by the UK to EU aggression. At the same time it is possible for UK exporters to have free access to the EU market without undermining the existing prices created by the customs union. While EU businesses would regret the loss of high preferential prices in the UK market, they would be against a vindictive response which would make matters worse for them.

A final concern is how accurate their model can be in assessing a major change in commercial relationships like leaving a customs union. The 'multilateral gravity model' they use, due to Costinot and Rodriguez-Clare (2013) (CR), assesses all countries' bilateral trade according to calculated bilateral elasticities which effectively 'sum up' the total ('general equilibrium') effects of the change. Thus CR argue that, if one is prepared to assume some set of 'micro-foundations' (that is, underlying relationships between consumers and producers, such as the state of competition), one can regard the gravity model as an accurate method to evaluate any shock to trade. At a theoretical level one can accept that, given a constant elasticity of trade response, an estimate of the effects of a tariff shock would be accurate. However, the question is whether one can regard such an elasticity as 'structural', that is invariant to the type of policy shock created. We discuss this in more detail in Chapter 4. The basic point is a simple one: an elasticity sums up the effect of a tariff on trade via many different channels, some of which reinforce each other, some of which offset each other. These channels will be activated to different degrees by different shocks. Therefore an elasticity that works when only one thing is disturbed, namely the product tariff, will differ when that disturbance is accompanied by many changes to other tariffs. In the case of a large shock to the structure of trade such as leaving a customs union, the elasticity will no doubt be quite different again. As CR point out, the difficulty lies in assessing the elasticities to use, and what we would add is that they are likely to vary with the nature of the joint shock imposed on the economy, and the effects of this on ambient features of the economy such as consumer prices, wages, and supplies of capital and of different types of labour.

Our model here, based on four sectors and four major 'countries' can reasonably be criticized as too aggregative to provide highly accurate estimates, yet it does have an explicit theoretical defence of the way it computes the equilibrium structure of industry and consumption; it at least is for sure a structural general equilibrium model, which can in principle evaluate any shock to the structure of trade or the economy. The gravity model may work well numerically, and be more accurate in detail, for quite general changes in conditions, like a general drop in transport costs, mirroring globalization, which is what CR use it for. The problem with using it for a shock to trade structure like the UK leaving a customs union is that the responses will certainly not be the same as for a general globalization shock; indeed such a shock changes the UK's internal structure substantially, in a way not assumed in a gravity model.

A further argument of Ottaviano et al. is that there would be 'dynamic' effects of leaving the EU, from reduced investment, technological diffusion, export learning effects, and investment in R&D. However, all these effects assume that there is no expansion in similar opposite effects as trade expands with the rest of the world. We see here again the omission of the general ROW effects of leaving a customs union. It must also be stressed that estimating these effects is difficult and uncertain; the empirical literature on growth is marked by much elaborate theory but considerable problems in 'identifying' the effects of growth mechanisms in practice.

Probably the most important element for the UK is the extent to which the UK state can establish favourable tax and regulation conditions for competition and entrepreneurship; because of this, in leaving the EU we avoid many damaging features of EU intervention and this will be beneficial, regardless of the structure of trade. Here recent work (Minford, 2015) has shown strong evidence that barriers to business affect UK growth. This is identified in Table 1.1 showing costs as a factor that could lower UK growth by some 0.5 per cent per annum, as a result of the dynamic effects on entrepreneurship of excessive regulation, especially in the labour market.

It is also said that we would no longer influence EU regulations, which is true. But we do not influence the regulations of any country to which we export and yet our exports are made to conform to them; this is part of our export costs, and our influence in the EU has little if any impact on these costs. But by leaving we avoid the massive cost of these regulations to our own production in general, as shown in Table 1.1. What will happen when we leave is that our exporters will have to continue to observe EU regulations on their products as they do now and as they do for all other countries to which they export; this is simply a normal cost of exporting anywhere. Also under the new suggested UK–EU treaty they could agree to continue to implement these regulations on all their production. As for everyone else (over 90 per cent of GDP) EU regulations will cease to be relevant, lifting both a current burden and a future threat.

It is true that the EU restrains UK politicians from self-damaging acts, such as subsidizing particular industries. However, politicians of most parties are now generally aware of the costs of such measures; and also the World Trade Organization (WTO) has become more effective in discouraging them. But in any case the costs of such particular actions are relatively minor.

Thus the costs to the UK of being in the EU, already high, are likely to increase under the pressure of the euro crisis. This implies that the case for leaving the EU will become even stronger, to the point where it overcomes the inertial force of the status quo. There is now definitely to be a referendum on whether to remain in the EU on whatever renegotiated terms this government is able to achieve. As can be seen from the figures above, the most desirable option is a new treaty with the EU that largely withdraws from EU joint arrangements but collaborates on particular issues of common interest, such as rights of migration, free capital movements, and possibly trade agreements on particular industries like cars where there is large-scale cross-investment. Of course political cooperation will continue in areas of mutual interest as with all our allies.

THE BOTTOM LINE: WHAT SHOULD BRITAIN DO IN THE LIGHT OF THESE COSTS?

When a country changes its institutions, as we are discussing here, we are in effect comparing outcomes over two contrasting long-term futures. The future of the UK in or out of the EU therefore involves two main sets of unknowns:

(1)   How would UK policies evolve outside the EU and how would they evolve inside?

(2)   What are the effects of these policy differences on UK performance?

To determine (1) we need to judge what UK policy would be outside the EU and what EU policy (as a key constraint on UK policy if it remained inside) would also be.

To determine (2) we need reliable models of policy effects.

Clearly both these requirements are hard to meet with any certainty. The resulting uncertainty has led some people to argue that the decision must be made on other, largely political grounds – that economics cannot in practice contribute to the debate.

Yet this is a non sequitur. For example in taking personal decisions about future careers we may lack any certainty about how each will turn out in terms of income, yet we do not as a result decide purely on grounds of our enjoyment of each career.

In the rest of this book we make assumptions about EU policies based on what they have been until now and also on the basis of statements of intent by the majority of EU governments, such as that of 'ever-closer union'. Faced with the crisis of the euro, euro-zone governments have made it clear that they will do 'whatever it takes' to maintain the euro in all participating countries; as the crisis has subsided they have committed themselves to much closer fiscal and banking union, as part of the overall agenda of ever-closer union. Some economists on this side of the Channel have been inclined to downplay this commitment and suggest that there would be, for example, a euro break-up, but there is every reason to believe that the statements represent real policy intentions, given that they have been systematically carried out so far.

We make assumptions about UK policies on similar grounds. UK political experience since 1979 has produced a broad consensus about the need for market-based policies; even the banking crisis has not in practice much disturbed this consensus, in spite of the fact that at one stage Labour under Ed Miliband seemed to wish to move away from it. This is not to say that UK policy follows some pure 'free market' model; like any country leaning more towards market-based policies, it has always had a fair amount of intervention and regulation moderating pure free market outcomes – as has the US also, to take another prominent example of a country that clearly leans towards free market solutions.

Perhaps the overriding consideration when one contemplates the different policies that could emerge from the EU versus those emerging from the UK on its own, is that the political economy of the two entities differs markedly. In the UK all of the policy agenda is under ongoing challenge, and the demands of vested interests for special treatment are closely scrutinized by a public process of evaluation and debate. In the EU, policy is made by a small elite, subject to little debate, and vested interest demands are often met behind closed doors, with little scrutiny by some open democratic debate. The European Parliament, which is supposed to be the equivalent of our national Parliament in creating effective scrutiny and debate, is a weak institution with little power and dominated itself by groups of MEPs whose interests do not lie in opposing vested interest demands (often the contrary), who back the elite-led process of the EU and who have neither the resources, the energy nor the inclination to hold the executive to account. Fundamentally it is this weakness in political economy that makes us expect a poor policy outcome from Brussels compared with Westminster.

These assumptions cover the most likely policy outcomes. Of course they may be wrong, and we can consider how we might insure against this happening. In practice, if they do turn out to be wrong, there are responses that would largely deal with the effects of a worsening if we were not in the EU, but these are to a high degree absent if we remain inside. UK institutions could change again, but EU institutions generally cannot be assumed to respond well, if at all. This embeds a further layer of argument about political economy: that just as the EU has relatively poor institutions for dealing with competing economic demands, so it has relatively inflexible institutions for dealing with changes in the economic environment.

What then of the models used to evaluate the effects? We have used models that are standard in international trade evaluations for the trade calculations and models of the economy that have been developed by ourselves and others for evaluating distortions to labour and product markets. The calculations they produce must be regarded as orders of magnitude designed to indicate a balance of advantage in each area and whether it is large or trivial.

Certain features of our results stand out. First, it is quite against the UK's interests to join the euro; as it happens, the UK negotiated an opt-out from the euro but since 'ever-closer union' includes being part of the euro, one can expect endless pressure to abandon this opt-out should we remain in the EU. Second, the UK would be better off with free trade, unbound by the EU's customs union policies. Third, it would be better off without EU regulation of the labour market and with its own regulations of product markets, especially those in finance.

To these economic findings that we contribute we can add some related points that are already well understood. First, control of immigration requires control of EU immigration, contrary to the EU stipulation of free movement. Second, the UK is not in favour of 'ever-closer union', the accepted description of the EU's long-term mission; not being in the euro, it will not participate in the proposed banking and fiscal union and it has not accepted the 'legal union' currently under discussion in the EU. Third, the City's ability to compete in world financial markets is a paramount UK interest best served by a UK-designed regulatory structure.

It seems rather obvious that there is no possible revision of the EU Treaties that could accommodate these UK interests. These treaties are designed for all members and they cannot be changed to allow one member to operate by different rules. In effect even a friendly government head such as Angela Merkel has made it quite clear that there is a strict limit on what treaty change is possible. One could summarize it this way: the UK would have allies for 'reforms' of EU practices (that is, movements towards more free trade and competition within the EU, such as liberalizing the service markets) but removal of the powers to regulate UK labour and product markets, to set customs union tariff and non-tariff barriers, and to enforce free movement are simply not negotiable, nor is the general objective of ever-closer union, including the joining of the euro.

At the same time one can find many areas of economic activity where the UK and the EU have common interests that could be well served by a variety of cooperative agreements. 'Leaving the EU' does not mean having nothing to do with the EU. Indeed it has been pointed out in his *Financial Times* articles by Wolfgang Munchau that the UK has effectively already left the EU in the practical sense that it is not in, nor has any intention of joining, the euro and has refused to subscribe to the longer-term aims of union. Nevertheless the UK does have a relationship with the EU. The question is how it can be modified in the best interests of both sides.

We can approach this question by thinking of a procedure under which, on a designated day, the UK leaves the EU formally at 9 am and then by 6 pm of the same day proclaims a plan to negotiate a fresh set of relationships with the EU that respect the UK interests set out above but that also provide for cooperation in areas of mutual advantage. Whether this would constitute some sort of 'membership' of the EU is a matter of semantics; it would be a new treaty relationship of the UK as a self-governing country with the EU as a group of close allies, quite different from the 'membership' relationship set out under the current general treaties and yet comparable with it in being a 'positive relationship' involving cooperation and mutual burdens in a wide variety of policy areas. Indeed, shorn of the endless recrimination and doubt that now encrusts our existing relationship with the EU, it could lead to much more proactive dialogue and to many more joint actions.

This new relationship should not be confused with some aggressive act. Existing members of the EU are highly conscious of the awkwardness for their own development, complete with the euro, of having the UK as a member that does not sign up to much of the core agenda, including the euro itself. What is required is a rewriting of the relationship so that this awkwardness is removed on both sides, leaving in its place a treaty of cooperation that brings definite gains to both sides.

Plainly in non-economic areas such as defence and foreign policy, cooperation already occurs outside the EU treaties through NATO, general diplomatic activity and legal agreements, such as on extradition. It is in the economic area where the EU has taken overriding powers that the UK wishes to remove and replace with selective cooperation. This embraces trade, regulation and immigration.

Trade

On trade the UK's interest is in free trade with the rest of the world and, if possible, with the EU. Because the WTO has been halted in its extension of general free trade by the failure of the Doha Round, some observers fear that by leaving the EU trade collective the UK would lay itself open to hostile commercial policy from the rest of the world and from the EU.

Yet the first point is that by removing the tariff and non-tariff barriers erected by the EU on its behalf, the UK would at once benefit from a large fall in import prices, a direct and obvious benefit to consumer living standards; we estimate this at around 10 per cent. The size of this effect may come as a shock given that there is much discussion of the EU single market's effects in promoting competition. However, what is not so widely recognized is the role of tariff and non-tariff barriers in raising the costs of imports and so reducing the spur of competition from abroad. According to our estimates the EU's tariff-equivalent of all protectionist measures is around 16 per cent.

The second point is that the UK would, on leaving, find that the prices at which it sold to other countries would be world prices. These are the prices that products obtain when sold to a randomly chosen country, taking as given existing commercial policies of the countries of the world. These policies affect the relative domestic prices of different products (that is, inside each country) and together with the GDP of each country determine total world demand for each product type; world demand and supply for that product type determines its world price. If the UK makes a product of that type, this will be the price it gets.

How do these prices differ from those that UK producers get inside the EU? For what they sell outside the EU there is no difference. But for what they sell inside the EU they get more, because of the protection created by the EU customs union. They lose this 'customs union premium' and this of course makes such UK producers oppose leaving the EU.

Hence we see the gainers from leaving are the consumers and firms who can buy at world prices, while the losers are the firms who gain from this premium, which they will now lose. Naturally therefore one should expect a strong campaign by these losing firms against leaving the EU. Yet the arithmetic of gains and losses overall is plain. Besides consumers, our gainer firms that inside the EU face higher prices on imports and on import-type and export-type home products, spend much more on them than our loser firms produce of them, even though these gainers tend not to realize this since it is a matter of obscure economics. On top of this net gain to our consumers and firms, there is the gain from moving resources away from industries in which we are inefficient to those where we are efficient and moving consumption to goods that are cheaper (but currently made expensive by protection). It is this calculation that underlies our finding in Chapter 4 that leaving the EU would bring a trade gain of around 4 per cent of GDP.

At this point people often express concerns. Will not non-EU countries erect barriers against our goods? Will we not face a barrier to selling in the EU?

What we need to understand is that if some other countries set up barriers against our trade, unlikely as that is, this would have no implications for the world prices of the types of products we produce. Those prices are set in all the markets of the world. If our producers faced some extra tariffs in some markets, this would have no effect on the world price of the goods we produce. The UK produces a small fraction of world exports in virtually all product markets. These UK exports will be more expensive in the markets with extra tariffs but the impact on the overall demand for these products will be negligible. Then what will happen to our exports in the markets where they face these tariffs? They will be diverted to markets where they do not. In the markets where we face tariffs, our competitors will sell the goods we did not sell; we will sell more in their other markets.

Given that world prices will be unaffected, our calculation holds exactly. This calculation estimates the gains of moving from protected EU prices on imports and exports to world prices on these.

This is not an easy idea to grasp for those not used to international trade theory. Most people think in terms of 'market access' and the bilateral bargaining between producers and the country to which they are selling. But this is not how world trade works – except in the very short run, which is soon over and so not relevant to a long-term shift like leaving the EU.

Consider a simple example: Jaguar cars. These have a certain price around the world as a brand of luxury car, competing closely with other luxury brands such as BMW, Mercedes, Porsche and Lexus. There is a world price of such luxury cars, by which we mean that Jaguar has to price its product competitively with all these other prices; world demand from upper middle class people around the world drives all these prices to the level at which this demand is equal to the world supply of these products. Now suppose that when the UK leaves the EU, say Thailand imposes a higher tariff on Jaguars. This would simply raise the Thai price; Jaguars will not sell less around the world nor would their price fall because any reduction of sales to Thailand would be easily absorbed by slightly higher sales in each of the many other markets where Jaguars are sold.

This illustrates what is known in international trade theory as the 'importance of being unimportant'; a small supplier in world markets such as the UK, faced with a tariff from country X, would simply divert supply to another market and so keep its price unchanged, passing the tariff on to the consumers in country X. The UK is too small to affect the world price of any product it sells – hence it is 'unimportant' at the world level.

This powerful argument implies that the calculation of the UK's net trade gains is immune to what third countries decide to do with their trade barriers on UK products, and is explicitly based on the assumption that the EU indeed raises its usual ('most favoured nation', MFN) trade barriers on UK products so that UK export prices in the EU market revert to world prices.

Let us consider further the question of what third country behaviour will actually be: of course few, if any, will raise tariffs against the UK. There are three main reasons why countries raise tariffs or non-tariff barriers. The first is to drive down the border prices of imports by reducing home demand; this is known as the 'optimal tariff' policy of using trade policy to improve the terms of trade. But as we have seen, no country has any 'monopoly power' over UK goods – that is, no ability to drive down UK prices – as the UK would simply divert them elsewhere at the same price.

The second reason countries raise tariffs is for the raising of revenue, especially in developing countries with low tax-raising capacity. But our leaving the EU has no effect on their desire to do this.

The third reason is the lobbying of home industries requiring protection, often on 'infant industry' grounds. But again the UK's relationship to the EU does not change this.

Some people are concerned that if we leave the EU we will be unable to influence the big trade agreement negotiations between the EU and the US or China. However, it is not at all clear that we want to be involved in such negotiations. Our aim is to sell the products we have at world prices wherever there is demand. These negotiations may raise or lower the world prices of our exports or those of our imports. But the outcome will be determined by the interests of many other countries; it is unclear how we could push them towards raising the prices of our exports and lowering the prices of our imports. Our diplomatic efforts are better spent on issues where we can have a useful effect.

By implication we have no particular interest in signing Free Trade Agreements with individual countries – even with China, which, as it happens, is much wedded to the idea of the WTO as a supranational keeper of trade peace. Like China, we too would have a strong interest in the WTO's role in this respect. We note in later chapters of this book how world trade has grown rapidly in spite of there being no Doha Round. It seems that multinational companies (MNCs) have created tariff competition much as they have created tax competition between different countries eager to obtain their investment in industry. Tariff competition works by the MNC offering to invest in industry at stage X of value-added in a country provided that country does not levy tariffs on its inputs or interfere with its exports. Stage X could be assembly; then the inputs could come from cheaper parts of the world, while the good assembled is exported all over the world. In effect this means that any tariff on imports of the assembled good into this country will have no effect on prices in the country because these are set by export prices in world markets – any rise in prices of the imported product would lead to them being undercut by exporters shifting product to the home market. By this method the MNC will have caused tariffs to be effectively extinguished on this industry in this country. Something like this must be happening for us to witness the massive growth of industrial intra-trade all over the Far East, for example. Even in the EU and the US we see that protection has been coming down steadily over the past few decades – similar forces are eroding protection there.

It is sometimes said that we should try to obtain a Free Trade Agreement with the EU. The problem about this is that with free trade the UK would enjoy lower prices on goods that are protected in the EU. If they levy on us the usual EU tariff-equivalent, then prices of UK exports to the EU would be brought up to EU levels and so the protection to EU producers would not be undermined. Hence it is natural to make the assumption that the EU levies its usual (MFN) tariff-equivalents on us when we leave. If we ask it not to, then in effect it seems we are asking to remain inside the customs union and are not leaving at all! However, in free trade agreements such as the North American Free Trade Agreement (NAFTA), different countries can have zero tariffs against their countries even while enjoying zero tariffs from other FTA partners; it may well be possible for the UK to negotiate such arrangements for particular industries that are highly integrated across the EU.

For example there are some industries where competition is heavily restricted, such as aerospace and airlines. In these examples existing markets are heavily organized between the UK, EU and other producers. In effect leaving the EU would leave these arrangements intact.

An example of a highly integrated industry is the volume car industry in which multinational companies have invested heavily on the assumption of a protected EU market. For such cases the drop in world prices would lead to heavy losses. An arrangement whereby the UK and the EU maintained zero tariffs and tariff-equivalents against each other would make much sense for this industry; effectively the EU market would maintain its existing prices and UK producers would continue to sell into this EU market at these prices, even though UK prices for cars would fall to world levels so that EU producers would lose their EU price premium in the UK market.

Failing that, given that the UK encouraged these investments, it could reasonably make some compensation when policy changes, on the usual basis that reform requires losers to be, if possible, compensated by gainers (in this case taxpaying households who enjoy lower consumer prices and other firms that enjoy lower input prices).

Alternatively, the existing arrangements for this industry could be left in place for a transitional period of a decade, allowing the industry time to adjust its capital stock and strategies to the new reality. This would mean that for a decade the current EU customs union protection would be continued by the UK for this industry only. The gain to the economy of this part of the trade regime change would be deferred for this decade, but then would be reaped like all the rest.

The first key point that emerges from this long discussion of trade is that, if we were outside the EU, the most important feature of UK traded output, whether exports or home products competing with imports, would be its 'competitiveness', that is, its 'value for money' as a product. If it were value for money, it would be bought all around the world and would displace foreign competition in the home market, whatever other countries may do in their trade policies.

The second key point is that certain industries will be worse off when EU protection is removed and they will lobby for transitional remedies, as well as for staying in the EU. In the well-worn way that accompanies supply-side reform they will have to be helped over the transition. But their opposition and transitional pain should not obscure the gains to the economy overall from lower prices of traded goods generally as we leave the EU and return to free world trade.

Regulation

Those defending EU regulations often argue that we are the cause of our own excess regulation because we 'gold-plate' EU regulations. Thus really, they argue, we cause the regulation and if we left the EU we would not change it, since we created it.

However, this is to misunderstand why we 'gold-plate' EU regulation. If there was no EU directive we would not have the regulation at all. But EU directives are fairly vague and imprecise. Our common law is, by contrast, extremely concrete and precise because it is derived from many cases of past law. Current application has to be argued from these precedents. Our statute law introduces new criteria into the law and so to operate alongside common law it has to generate equivalent precision, otherwise it cannot be used effectively in UK courts which will not rule on the basis of unclear and vague pronouncements. Thus our civil service lawyers have to take EU directives and turn them into precise and workable law; this involves carefully going through all the contingencies in which they might apply and saying what exactly they mandate. None of this is necessary on the continent where only statute law prevails and is interpreted by judges with wide powers.

Unfortunately this EU-directive-created law introduces much extra complexity into our law. This would not be there without EU directives.

Evaluating all this EU regulation is a huge task and our approach has been to take the salient interventions that distort markets. These are mainly interventions in the labour market, inspired by 'social' and 'human rights' considerations. In product markets the situation is complex. In some markets EU regulation may not be notably different from regulations thrown up by domestic regulators; furthermore the EU is pro-competitive in its policy philosophy, as can be seen in the Competition Directorate. But there is still a general problem with having regulation coordinated by a central EU authority: it creates intense lobbying by the firms in each industry and tends to favour dominant producers who can lobby most effectively. A recent example is vacuum cleaners, where James Dyson has protested against the large German industry's success in setting a high ceiling on vacuum cleaners' energy consumption; according to Dyson this is anti-competitive, favouring the dominant German industry against newer competitors. There is also the salient case of financial markets in which EU regulators are distrustful of major competitive processes, there is populist dislike of financiers, and most EU countries have industries with poor ability to compete against the City of London and hence propose measures that would reduce its competitive edge. The latest proposal for a Financial Transactions Tax has emerged out of such factors.

The difficulty in costing these regulative interventions in labour and product markets is to know how in practice they will be applied, by regulators and by the courts. However, in essence all these interventions constitute a tax on business activity financing a transfer to some beneficiary, a particular class of worker or a particular class of consumer. This tax in turn reduces economic activity and employment (if it does not reduce the number of people wanting to work it will increase unemployment; but often when employment falls the relevant job-losers leave the labour market). It does so by raising the country's relative costs in world markets or 'competitiveness' because the tax cannot be shifted back onto labour or other inputs by lowering wage and other input prices; the reason is that unemployment benefits and minimum wages prevent wages from falling while other input prices are generally set in world markets.

The models we have used here only cost the one-off effect on activity and so on. However, there may also be an effect on growth itself, which therefore causes an accumulating loss of activity and employment; this effect persists as long as the tax remains. This 'dynamic' effect is now the focus of policy interest and we have used a new model developed by Minford (2015) to contribute a tentative estimate of this effect too.

Estimating the effects of regulation is made difficult by the need to calculate the 'tax-equivalent' of the regulation: namely what cost it imposes on the businesses regulated and how the 'revenue', or gains, from the regulation are distributed. If the gains are distributed in a 'lump sum' manner so that there are no incentive effects on recipients' behaviour, then we can disregard the latter. But the costs on business will almost certainly affect business incentives; calculating them requires a substantial amount of research on the details of the businesses involved. In the case of regulation of labour markets, again, it is a matter of calculating how they affect business incentives, but in this case there will also be key incentive effects on workers.

In two major product areas the impact of EU regulation either has been or threatens to be massive: energy and finance. In energy the EU is mandating extremely high targets for 'renewable' energy such as from wind and sun; here the costs have been large and well-known (Congdon, 2014a). In finance the UK has now ceded final regulative authority to the EU; given the EU majority countries' hostility to financial activity for the reasons mentioned above, we have considerable reason to fear substantial negative effects from their future policies (Congdon, 2014b).

In labour markets the EU's interventions have been going on for a long time, ever since the era of Jacques Delors and the inauguration of the 'Social Market'. The UK insisted on an opt-out from the Social Chapter but, having signed up to the Single Market, it was forced to limit working hours on the grounds that this was a 'health and safety' matter coming within the scope of Single Market rules. Then when Labour came into power in 1997, it soon surrendered the opt-out from the Social Chapter, ushering in many more EU labour market interventions, including 'TUPE' (giving unions protection of their previous arrangements under privatization), maternity and paternity rights, contract rights, and rights for part-timers.

In our evaluation of the effects of all these measures, we have used the Liverpool Model, which was one of the first UK models to have a 'supply side' built to assess them. The fact that the range of estimates is wide is inevitable, given the difficulty of assessing exactly how much all these tax-equivalents are. The general point is that the EU is a highly interventionist organization, with a strong bias in favour of 'top-down' regulation and a mind-set that is 'socialist' in the sense that it favours action to force what it sees as direct gains for classes of people regardless of their market consequences. This philosophy is not necessarily accompanied by demands for public ownership and the opposition to private business or to privatization that is associated with explicit socialism, though it is in the cases of some politicians; it is usually described as 'social democracy', but unfortunately its economic effects are still damaging.

Immigration

The fury of a wide swathe of UK voters with the loss of control of immigration is a major new element in the UK debate since this book's first edition. It is a major game-changer, since while voters have some understanding of economic costs, they tend to relegate them in importance as irritants that can be absorbed rather than as being allowed to cause major institutional changes.

Leaving the EU would enable the UK government to apply the same criteria to EU immigrants as they do to non-EU immigrants. This does not mean there would necessarily be fewer immigrants overall; rather it would imply that an economic test would be applied to all immigrants and the balance of immigration altered towards immigrants with defined and required skills and with defined familial links to existing UK citizens.

This rebalancing of immigrants away from the unskilled would defuse the fury of voters referred to above. This fury has built up because unskilled immigrants have had damaging effects on poor, unskilled UK citizens; essentially these people's jobs and communities have been greatly affected, even if nationally UK employment has gone up to absorb the immigration and for other people these immigrants have brought advantages (for example in supplying low-wage services cheaply).

We have not allowed for this rebalancing of immigration to cause any economic cost or benefit. Arguably it should cause a benefit since the immigrants would become more skilled and this could create greater spill-over effects for UK citizens. However, we have not attempted to quantify this. What is clear is that it totally contravenes the EU freedom of move-ment of peoples and is incompatible with EU membership; it cannot be an object of 'negotiation'. This EU freedom may or may not be necessary for the EU's economic objectives, but it is certainly central to the political definition of the EU as a process of ever-closer union, to a federal state to which, of course, free movement is integral.

It must be stressed that this creation of controls on all immigration would not be a policy to 'stop immigration from the EU'. Rather it would subject all immigration to the same criteria, on which the UK has traditionally – at least until the recent fury created by inability to control EU migration – been rather liberal in its approach. Many people of UK origin and with UK associations exist all around the world and many have been admitted to the UK, notably from old colonies such as East Africa or Hong Kong. UK business and universities have also in practice been largely free to recruit the highly skilled labour they needed. Nor has this ever been controversial. What did become controversial was massive immi-gration from the poorer countries of the EU in the last decade and a half; this, together with some cases of false asylum often involved with terror-ism, has soured UK public opinion on immigration, to the point where it is not possible to see any remedy except the imposition of controls on EU labour.

POLICY CONCLUSIONS

In the first edition of this book it was possible to argue that there was some room for doubt about the desirability of the UK leaving the EU. Maybe the EU would improve or maybe UK policies would deteriorate so that the long-term balance of advantage could swing back to remaining.

This is no longer possible, in the light of two main factors. First, the EU's approach to economics has decidedly worsened and is continuing to do so under the impact of the euro crisis, which rumbles on unstoppably. The second factor is the emergent political hostility to the key economic interest of the UK in its large financial sector. As we can now see, these poor economic policies follow essentially from the poor political economy of the EU, dominated as it is by vested interests.

Allowing for these factors in our calculations makes it impossible to suggest any doubt that economically the UK would enjoy greatly improved prospects outside the EU. As we have already noted, many of the fears expressed about trade or business are the result either of misunderstanding or of pure self-interest on the part of those benefiting from EU protectionism or other interventionist measures.

Unfortunately such economic arguments on their own do not carry much weight with a general public suspicious of abstract argument. However, the politics of the EU question have now been changed by the rise of the immigration issue on the back of unfettered entry from the EU by migrants from poorer countries. While the well-to-do may sneer that such an issue does not reflect the overall net benefits of poor immigrants, it does reflect the anxieties of many poorer UK citizens who feel the direct impact of these arrivals on their jobs, communities and public goods. In practice the only way to resolve this issue is to rebalance EU immigration towards the more skilled and to restore control of total EU immigration to the UK government – this cannot be done without leaving the EU.

So it turns out that just as the EU's economic policies have become most threatening to UK interests, political developments from EU migration have made it likely that the UK would decide in a referendum to leave the EU. The politics and economics may well have converged.

WHAT IS IN THE REST OF THIS BOOK

The remaining chapters of this book divide into two main parts. The next three chapters consider in detail the costs and benefits of the key aspects of remaining in the EU: regulation, joining the euro, and trade. They provide the analytic and empirical back-up for the costs set out in this opening chapter. The next part consists of the final three chapters, which provide a detailed account of the facts and the associated literature on trade, respectively in agriculture, manufacturing and services. These chapters provide the background for our overall evaluation of the trade costs in Chapter 4; they can be read separately, as Chapter 4 sums up the findings from them that are relevant to the cost–benefit calculation it makes.

All views expressed in this book are personal to the authors and are in no way related to those of the organizations they are affiliated to.

2. The costs of EU regulation

The power of the EU to regulate product and labour markets comes from the Single Market arrangement of the mid-1980s. This gave powers to the Commission, with the agreement of the EU governing council of member states under Qualified Majority Voting, to issue directives in these matters. The greatest irony about this arrangement is that it was forced through the EU by a coalition of the UK and Germany; Mrs Thatcher's UK government of the time was particularly enthusiastic about what it saw as a spreading of competition across all EU markets; Jacques Delors, the EU Commission President, used this enthusiasm cleverly to get the measure through against much socialist resistance from other countries.

The UK government was naive in thinking the measure would work to spread competition. What we now know is that M. Delors promised the resisting governments a socialist arrangement to 'compensate' for the pressures from the Single Market. No sooner was the Single Market adopted than he announced the creation of a Social Chapter of the Treaties that would ensure the Single Market satisfied social objectives. While the UK negotiated an opt-out from the Social Chapter, outraged at what it saw as a betrayal of the Single Market vision, in due course Tony Blair's Labour government of 1997 gave away this opt-out, apparently in a bid to promote an image of the UK as 'pro-European', though also tacitly agreeing with much of the social agenda. But in any case, even with the opt-out, the Single Market's health and safety provisions were used to put a cap on UK working hours, a major restriction on the workings of the labour market. Once the opt-out went, a great raft of labour market intervention in the UK followed; these included 'TUPE' (giving unions protection of their previous arrangements under privatization), enhanced maternity and new paternity rights, rights for part-timers equivalent to those for full-timers, equal pay for women and 'minorities', and rights for unions and workers of 'full consultations' before factories could be closed or redundancies made. The interventions have so far stopped short of imposing on the UK the full gamut of union-friendly arrangements usual on the continent but there can be no certainty they will not be forced in over time. Qualified Majority Voting implies that the UK is potentially outvoted on all issues to do with the Single Market where the continent follows a different philosophy from it. Qualified Majority Voting does not so far apply to harmonization of social security and social protection policies; however, one can have no confidence that it will not eventually be extended to cover this too.

In what follows, we review first the labour market regulations where the most intrusive general interventions from the EU occur. Second we look at product market regulation where there is a particularly strong threat to the major UK markets in the City as well as a general tendency to push up costs to 'harmonize' standards across the EU; such harmonization effectively is set to reduce competition with the EU's dominant producers in each industry.

2.1   LABOUR MARKET REGULATION IN THE EU

It is clear that labour market institutions in the rest of the EU are hostile to job creation. This is not just our view here but that of the OECD. It is also well evidenced by the high levels of unemployment throughout the EU for some years, of course now exacerbated by the euro-zone crisis.

Thus the OECD has for years conducted surveys of the extent of labour market 'protection', by which it means barriers to hiring and firing workers. These surveys (where the index runs from 0 to 6: the higher the value the higher the burden) are based largely on responses by employers to questionnaires about the burdens they see imposed by regulation. The latest 2013 survey is reproduced in Table 2.2. It can be seen that the UK is substantially less protectionist than other EU countries, in spite of the general pressure from Social Chapter principles. Nevertheless it is more protectionist than the US, and this arguably reflects this pressure to date. In a recent report for the Prime Minister (Beecroft, 2012), the venture capitalist Adrian Beecroft pointed out that in a wide variety of ways the UK was failing to give businesses enough freedom in their labour relations and that this was contributing to slowing the growth of jobs in the UK. Fortunately, in spite of this, UK jobs growth has been satisfactory, though we remain below full employment, and participation in the labour market by specific groups of workers, such as women, the young, older workers and disabled workers, remains disappointing.

What remains a particular concern is how far this pressure could go in the future. The EU Social Chapter favours strong powers for unions as well as invasive regulations on hiring and firing. Were the UK to be pressured into reaching the sort of environment prevailing in some other parts of the EU, the results would be dramatic. In an exercise to compute these possibilities using the Liverpool Model of the UK, we carried out simulations of what they might do, which are reproduced in Table 2.1.

Table 2.1   The effects on UK output and unemployment of EU-style social measures

I. A minimum wage

where wage is	(a) 50% of male median	(b) 2/3 of average
Long-term effects on:		
Output (%)	−1.5	−5.0
Unemployment		
% of labour force	+1.8	+5.0
million	+0.5	+1.4

II. Union power simulation

	Union power rises	
	(a) to mid-1980s level	(b) to 1980 level
Long-term effects on:		
Output (%)	−3.0	−5.8
Unemployment		
% of labour force	+1.3	+4.3
million	+0.4	+1.3

III. Rise in the social cost burden on employers

	(a) by 20% of wages	(b) by 60% of wages
Long-term effects on:		
Output (%)	−4.4	−11.0
Unemployment		
% of labour force	+3.0	+18.0
million	+0.9	+5.5

IV. Combination of minimum wages, union power rise, and higher social cost burdens on employers (combination of I–III, (a) and (b))

	Least	Most
Long-term effects on:		
Output (%)	−9.0	−20.0
Unemployment		
% of labour force	+10.0	(extreme value)
million	+3.0	(extreme value)

Source: Minford (1998, p. 200); simulations based on Liverpool Model of UK.

It can be seen that these are large costs, even in the least-cost scenario with its cost at 9 per cent of GDP and 10 per cent on unemployment. The high-cost scenario is obviously hugely damaging, at 20 per cent of GDP and an unquantifiable rise in unemployment.

What exactly was the effect of EU membership and specifically the introduction of the Social Chapter on the UK? We can use the general OECD series on employment protection to give us an idea. From 1985 to 1999 the value was 1.032; from 2000 to 2012 it rose and stayed at 1.198, nearly a 20 per cent rise. This can be associated with the effects of new measures brought in after the Social Chapter became binding on the UK in 1997. In 2013 the coalition government acted on the Beecroft Report and brought in a package of measures on issues where the Social Chapter was not binding, which reduced the value back to 1.032. What we can see from this is that we have so far been able to maintain a reasonably liberal order in the labour market in spite of the Social Chapter. However, the situation is constantly shifting with new decisions by the European Court and new directives from the Commission. So far it seems we have been able to offset one set of regulative measures with another later set of liberalizing ones. Nevertheless, the Chapter can be seen in itself to have raised the index by nearly 20 per cent. The measures involved are listed in the Beecroft Report; they include TUPE, which protected union employees against dismissal by the new company after a privatization, extended rights for temporary workers, provisions for extended consultation over closures and dismissals, and numerous directives on worker rights of all sorts. They do not include self-inflicted interventions like the introduction of the minimum wage.

Table 2.1, showing effects of different degrees of EU intervention, is just an illustration of possibilities. Clearly some parts have already been enacted. But the key point is that, as we look forward and try to predict how 'ever-closer union' might work out for us with our traditions of relatively free markets, we cannot have much confidence in what could happen within the EU, given that our partners, who can dominate the agenda via Qualified Majority Voting, have quite different labour market institutions and approaches, which can be briefly summarized as being corporatist or socialist ('social democratic', favouring regulation rather than ownership as the means to achieve social objectives).

2.2 PRODUCT MARKET REGULATION

The original idea for the regulation of EU product markets was that each country would have its own regulations and from the resulting regulative competition would emerge some convergence towards a more general and effective system. This idea did not last long in the face of demands from industry protagonists for a 'level playing field'; leading firms in each sector feared that firms in other countries could be advantaged by a different, less intrusive regulatory system. There could be a 'race to the bottom'

Table 2.2   OECD measures of labour market intervention scale from 0 (least restrictions) to 6 (most restrictions)

	Protection of permanent workers against individual and collective dismissals	Protection of permanent workers against (individual) dismissal	Specific requirements for collective dismissal	Regulation on temporary forms of employment
	EPRC	EPR	EPC	EPT
Austria	2.44	2.12	3.25	2.17
Belgium	2.95	2.08	5.13	2.42
Denmark	2.32	2.10	2.88	1.79
Estonia	2.07	1.74	2.88	3.04
Finland	2.17	2.38	1.63	1.88
France	2.82	2.60	3.38	3.75
Germany	2.98	2.72	3.63	1.75
Greece	2.41	2.07	3.25	2.92
Hungary	2.07	1.45	3.63	2.00
Ireland	2.07	1.50	3.50	1.21
Luxembourg	2.74	2.28	3.88	3.83
Netherlands	2.94	2.84	3.19	1.17
Norway	2.31	2.23	2.50	3.42
Poland	2.39	2.20	2.88	2.33
Portugal	2.69	3.01	1.88	2.33
Slovak Republic	2.26	1.81	3.38	2.42
Slovenia	2.67	2.39	3.38	2.50
Spain	2.28	1.95	3.13	3.17
Sweden	2.52	2.52	2.50	1.17
Switzerland	2.10	1.50	3.63	1.38
United Kingdom	1.62	1.12	2.88	0.54
United States	1.17	0.49	2.88	0.33
OECD unweighted average	2.29	2.04	2.91	2.08

Notes: Data refer to 1 January 2013 for OECD countries and Latvia; 1 January 2012 for other countries. Only version 3 indicators are reported. Data updated to 1 May 2013 for Slovenia and the United Kingdom are available at: http://www.oecd.org/els/emp/EPLtimeseries.xlsx.

Source: OECD Employment Protection Database, 2013 update.

in regulatory laxness; dominant firms would then face easier entry from rivals. They lobbied for a high and equal level of regulation, a 'level playing field'; standards would be 'raised' across the industry, preventing competitors from entering the market with different products.

Table 2.3   Product market regulation: OECD measures

	Product market regulation			
	1998	2003	2008	2013
Austria	2.12	1.61	1.37	1.19
Belgium	2.30	1.64	1.52	1.39
Czech Republic	2.64	1.88	1.50	1.39
Denmark	1.66	1.48	1.35	1.22
Estonia	–	–	1.37	1.29
Finland	1.94	1.49	1.34	1.29
France	2.38	1.77	1.52	1.47
Germany	2.23	1.80	1.41	1.29
Greece	2.75	2.51	2.21	1.74
Hungary	2.66	2.11	1.54	1.33
Iceland	2.03	1.62	1.48	1.50
Italy	2.36	1.80	1.49	1.26
Luxembourg	–	1.60	1.44	1.46
Netherlands	1.82	1.49	0.96	0.92
Norway	1.87	1.56	1.54	1.46
Poland	3.19	2.42	2.04	1.65
Portugal	2.59	2.12	1.69	1.29
Slovak Republic	–	2.17	1.61	1.33
Slovenia	–	–	1.89	1.70
Spain	2.39	1.79	1.59	1.44
Sweden	1.89	1.50	1.61	1.52
Switzerland	2.49	1.99	1.55	1.50
United Kingdom	1.32	1.09	1.20	1.08
United States	1.50	1.30	1.11	–

Measuring this excess regulation is difficult. Fortunately, as in the case of labour market regulation, the OECD has devoted a lot of resources to surveys measuring the regulatory barriers created by governments. In Table 2.3 we reproduce the OECD's overall product market regulation index.

It is interesting to see that the level of regulatory burdens recorded by business has gone down throughout the EU since 1998. Nevertheless in the UK it has hardly changed, falling very slightly over the period to 2008 and dropping a bit further since then. It remains below every other EU country, other than the Netherlands, which has for long had a pro-business culture.

This index is made up of a host of sub-indices; the UK's relative attractiveness to business is widely spread across the three main categories of sub-index: state control, barriers to entrepreneurship and barriers to trade

Table 2.4   Business regulation index, Economic Freedom of the World, 2012

Austria	6.2
Belgium	6.2
Denmark	6.9
France	6.2
Germany	6.6
Ireland	7.0
Italy	5.5
Luxembourg	7.1
Netherlands	6.9
Spain	6.0
US	6.7
UK	7.0

Source: Fraser Institute (Gwartney et al., 2012).

and investment. Thus it would seem that EU membership has not obviously damaged the UK's performance in business regulation and that the Single Market is in this respect functioning reasonably well. One caveat is in order: if the regulations are written to please the dominant producers in each product area, they might well express satisfaction even if the consumer is less well served. However, as there is no survey of consumer opinion, and indeed it would be hard for consumers to judge such industrial matters, we have no evidence on this point. What evidence we have from industry therefore does support the idea that harmonized regulation works well.

The Fraser Institute in Canada, in cooperation with other free market think tanks around the world, compiles another measure of business regulation burdens; here the index is on a scale of 0–10, and as it rises the burden is falling (see Table 2.4).

The picture is not very different in its current level from that given by the OECD surveys. Again the UK is close to the top of the ranking and apparently none the worse for being in the EU. However, the Institute has measured UK levels of business regulation since 2000, when it was 8.17. Since then it has dropped to 7.6 in 2005, fallen further to 6.8 in 2010, and only recently in 2012 picked up slightly to 7.0. These scores out of 10 are not terrible, but overall we observe a drop of around 14 per cent over the period: again we are likely to be seeing here the effect of increased regulative activity by the EU since the UK governments of Messrs Blair, Brown and Cameron were not in favour of increased business regulation.

We should note that because the rest of the EU is in general more burdensome in its regulations, this remains a pressure point from the UK's viewpoint, in that other countries may not be averse to the UK introducing greater regulatory burdens, to avoid its having a competitive advantage. This temptation for other EU countries, burdened by high regulatory costs, to raise UK costs in order to reduce the effects on their own competitiveness is endemic.

One area of regulation where a visible and substantial cost is being incurred is the EU's climate change agenda on renewables. This is estimated to be costing the economy, mainly directly charged for in fuel bills, some 2 per cent of GDP (Congdon, 2014a). Renewable energy in the UK is high cost, even more so than elsewhere because of the vagaries of wind and sun; its costs are compounded by the need to back up these energy supplies with more reliable sources. Whatever the merits of the climate change agenda, these high costs indicate that there are more cost-effective ways to pursue it.

Another area where UK interests are seriously threatened by EU regulation is the City of London. Here the overall regulation has since 2014 been placed in EU hands. Apart from placing a cap on staff bonuses and proposing a Financial Transactions Tax (still being fought over), the EU regulators have not yet moved on the new framework. Tim Congdon (2014b) has recently written on the outlook for this and concluded that it constitutes a serious threat to the City's future functioning. The problem with this area of business is that the rest of the EU have been mostly hostile to UK – and US – style finance and banking, which does not prevail anywhere else in the EU, apart from the Netherlands, Ireland and Luxembourg to a moderate extent. Plainly the City of London is a major UK industry, contributing some 10 per cent of UK GDP; for it to be regulated by a hostile EU process is a matter of great concern.

We cannot cost this threat in any sensible way. In our table of potential costs due to regulation (Table 2.1) we may think of this threat as contributing to the higher end of the cost range. Essentially the UK faces in respect of this regulation, as with labour market and product market regulation, a substantial range of uncertainty, given the existence of Qualified Majority Voting. The other countries of the EU share an approach to these matters that is generally in favour of more rather than less regulation; like many with an essentially socialist political outlook, regulation offers them the gains of intervention without any fiscal cost and it is therefore highly tempting. One can be quite unsure how this will play out over a few decades of further EU membership. So far these problems may have been patched up to a reasonable extent, judging from the indicators we have examined. However, the proclaimed aim of the EU is ever-closer union, effectively a state with a strong top-down central power. Even if pro-EU politicians in the UK have proclaimed repeatedly that we should not take this aim seriously, it has been apparent in practice that it is deadly serious, as the actions to implement it have rolled out. It follows that ultimately the resulting top-down regulative structure that would emerge would consistently violate the UK's traditional free market approach.

2.3   GROWTH AND REGULATION

So far we have examined the one-off permanent costs of regulation on the UK. However, there has been increasing concern with 'dynamic' effects of such measures; by this is meant the effects on growth. Such dynamic effects implicitly rise over time in that growth is stunted by them. Plainly such potential costs are therefore extremely serious. However, it has proved difficult to find evidence of causal linkages between either regulation or associated business costs due, for example, to taxation, and growth. There have been many studies showing that there is a statistical link between the two, but causation cannot be demonstrated by such studies.

In recent research (Minford, 2015) evidence of causation has been established. A model of the UK economy in which regulatory costs affect productivity growth is simulated to generate behaviour of GDP and productivity, as well as other economic variables over the period from 1970 to 2009. If this model is a correct representation of the UK then the behaviour of the economy we actually observed in this period should be accounted for by these simulations. This work finds that one cannot reject this hypothesis statistically with 95 per cent confidence.

This work represents something of a breakthrough in the longstanding debate over causal evidence in this area. The specific effect of a sustained ten-year 5 per cent rise in the measure of intervention (equivalent to a rise in the effective tax rate) on growth is for a fall in growth of 1.5 per cent a year over two decades. This is a substantial effect, which tends to dwarf the other effects in this book. It means, for example, that if the EU were to raise the implicit tax represented by its regulatory interventions by an average of 1.7 per cent over the next decade, by 2035 the UK would be some 10 per cent poorer. Unfortunately such a rise seems entirely possible given the parameters within which 'ever-closer union' would operate, allowing harmonization of all areas of tax and regulation along the lines of the general continental model; indeed it could well be a gross underestimate.

2.4   CONCLUSIONS

Central to the functioning of any economy is its regulative regime; this acts as a complement to the tax regime in establishing how business-friendly and pro-competitive the environment is. A regime that permits cheap entry for new businesses and low ongoing costs of doing business encourages competition and so innovation. Though the 'Single Market' in regulation is often extolled as a model of a 'level playing field' that encourages competition, what is found in surveys of business opinion is that product regulation in the EU is intrusive and may favour large incumbents, while labour market regulation doles out rights for workers that are expensive for employers to honour, that discourage employment and deter business expansion. We may also note that business taxation itself varies markedly across EU countries and is not yet 'harmonized'; however, for the UK with its relatively low marginal tax rates on business and high earners, there could also exist a threat under 'ever-closer union' that this too could be jeopardized. Using the Liverpool Model of the UK, with its pioneering treatment of the supply side, we have found that there are high potential costs to the economy from a large-scale extension of EU regulation. On top of these one-off ('static') costs, such an extension also threatens substantial potential 'dynamic' costs (that is, reductions in the UK's growth rate). The remedy for these threats is a new treaty in which EU product regulations only apply to the sectors exporting to the EU, and non-product (for example, labour) regulations do not apply at all. The UK would then be free to choose its own regulative non-product regime and decide case by case on what product regimes it would adopt for products not exported to the EU.

3. The cost of the euro

In this chapter we consider the costs of the euro for the UK (and the related issue of bail-out costs); this is a major cost of being in the EU since it is now mandatory for members of the EU to join the euro at some time. While the UK currently has an opt-out from the euro, this is inconsistent with the general objective for the EU of 'ever-closer union'. Like our opt-out from the Social Chapter, which we were always under pressure to abandon in the interests of European unity and was abandoned by Labour after obtaining power in 1997, the euro opt-out is not envisaged by our EU partners as being viable in the long term. Past experience has shown that the way the EU evolves is something over which we have little control. So we assume here that if we stay in the EU we will eventually agree to join the euro.

We begin with some discussion of how the introduction of the euro has derailed the EU project and led to endemic crisis. The euro, as we have seen, has therefore become costly for those in the EU who have so far joined it.

We then go on to consider in detail how the UK's interests are affected by joining the euro.

3.1   EU AND THE EURO

The European Union was originally founded after the Second World War as the European Coal and Steel Community, with the aim of generating such economic cooperation in Europe that wars between European countries would be impossible. The founders, such as Jean Monnet, always intended that one step would lead to another on the road to 'ever-closer union', the ultimate aim of the latest Lisbon Treaty, where it is now explicitly stated as such.

Until the recent crisis of the euro, the progress of this project was solid, even spectacular. What had begun as an agreement about coal and steel had become, in roughly half a century, 'the European Union', with the Lisbon Treaty embedding all the substance of a new European Constitution that had been sought when the draft Constitution was put before the constituent countries and rejected in France and the Netherlands by referendums – thus effectively a new multi-country State. Most extraordinarily, none of this progress had been generally agreed in any democratic way. Indeed, as we have seen, when democratic agreement was sought to the draft Constitution, it was not granted. The progress was achieved by agreement between governments which knew that they could not necessarily get their own people to subscribe to it. It was, in the most direct sense of the word, an elite project, where a cross-European elite determined what would be done and then pushed it through without popular consultation.

The project has now stumbled badly; the reason is the adoption of the euro, which was the cause of the major crisis now assailing the EU and specifically the majority euro-zone part of it. Whereas other countries around the world began recovering from the banking crisis during 2009 and by 2014 were well on the way to recovery, the euro-zone plunged into the euro crisis in 2010 and is still barely recovering from it. During the four years since the euro crisis occurred, the EU and its euro-zone members in particular have put together numerous policies designed to halt the crisis. There have been the tripartite bail-outs involving the EU Commission (and euro-zone governments), the ECB and the IMF (the 'troika'). There has been the Target 2 implicit lending programme via the ECB. Then there was Outright Monetary Transactions, the declaration by the ECB President, Mario Draghi, to do 'whatever it took' to save the euro, meaning that he would buy (or, strictly, arrange to have bought by commercial banks, since the ECB was not allowed to do so) government bonds being threatened by massive sales in whatever quantity was needed to stabilize their prices. Most recently the ECB announced two rounds of new measures to counter deflation: the first involving negative interest rates on bank balances at the ECB and a subsidy to bank costs for banks hitting lending targets; the second involving large purchases of private bonds to inject money into the banking system. Most recently it has resorted to Quantitative Easing (QE) as undertaken by the US Fed and the Bank of England. Through all this the politicians of the euro-zone have remained adamant that the euro would be saved at whatever cost. They also seem to have persuaded the peoples of countries which might have considered leaving the euro that this would be a mistake, judging by opinion polls in Greece and Spain for example, and the weak progress of anti-euro parties in Germany. So it would seem that unless politics in the euro-zone takes a quite unprecedented turn, the euro will survive whatever happens.

Unfortunately the euro-zone is now stagnating, unemployment remains at record levels, youth unemployment at extraordinary levels, and wages and prices are threatening deflation. And what is the reason for this terrible turn of events? It is nothing but the euro because this has removed from national politicians in the euro-zone a key power of adjustment to shocks, namely the power to let the exchange rate move.

The risk of removing this adjustment power was well-known to the EU politicians that pushed through the euro project to its start in 1999. The two key men who did this were Helmut Kohl and François Mitterrand, and their decision to do it was fatefully tied up with the fall of the Berlin Wall and subsequent German reunification. Reunification was a project about which many countries were nervous; the UK was one and there was opposition in many countries among particular groups remembering the policies pursued when Germany was last united before the Second World War. Mitterrand pledged France's support but in return he demanded that the Deutsche Mark (DM) and the Bundesbank that ran it be replaced by a euro run by a pan-European central bank; his idea was that this would reduce German dominance of the European economy. Of course Mitterrand had had experience of German dominance when forced into a U-turn on his expansionary policies in the early 1980s. Desperate for support, Kohl gave him support for the euro in return for his support on reunification. Both duly went ahead, as within the EU the Franco-German axis when in operation is irresistible.

This account reveals that the project was essentially political. Any economic problems the euro might cause were treated as secondary by both men. When the so-called 'economists' who opposed the euro trotted out the usual arguments about 'optimal currency areas' and the difficulties of stabilizing 'asymmetric country shocks' without floating exchange rates, the 'monetarists' countered that a unified European State would be built because of the pressures of such problems: 'Europe' would be created '*par la monnaie*' (by monetary unification).

Unfortunately for the 'monetarists' what the euro crisis has revealed is that a European State is very far from having been created by the euro-zone's problems and that the 'solutions' being cobbled together for the euro crisis are being produced by nation-states through gritted teeth. For its first decade there were no particular problems with the euro because the economic environment was so benign; the 'noughties' were a period of strong world growth until 2007 and it was not until the end of 2008 that the banking crisis exploded with the Lehman collapse. It then took a couple of years before the fiscal deficits in southern Europe developed as a result of the Great Recession. When these deficits provoked speculative attack on euro-zone countries in 2010, there was no EU or euro-zone mechanism in place to help them. Indeed the ECB was explicitly forbidden by the Maastricht Treaty from buying government bonds. So as the asymmetric shocks rained down on southern euro-zone countries, they were powerless to resist them except through attempted deflation. Yet these policies were not successful in stopping speculative attack; indeed they fuelled further speculation that the unpopularity of deflation might trigger departure from the euro. This led to further attack on these countries' government bond markets since these were the main investment vehicles that would suffer in value if they left the euro.

It is hard to create a model of all the countries involved in the euro because there are so many and the complications of each economy are considerable. There has been a fair bit of work attempting to analyse the effects of monetary union on the economic behaviour of euro-zone countries but the challenges involved have made this work rather inconclusive; a further factor has been that these countries had decided anyway to join the euro and this created pressures on economists of these countries (who had the biggest incentives to do the work) to pull their punches in view of the possible consequences for their careers. By contrast, a high-profile debate was started by the UK government about whether the UK should join the euro and this gave rise to a substantial volume of work, the consensus of which was that there could be large costs for economic stability of losing the pound. Against this there were found to be potential micro-economic benefits from eliminating currency uncertainty against the euro; however, it was recognized that there could be offsetting costs if euro entry gave rise to greater currency fluctuations against the dollar in which the bulk of our other trade was conducted.

In the next section of this chapter we examine in detail the costs and benefits for the UK of joining the euro since this is now considered to be an inevitable long-run consequence of remaining in the EU; 'ever-closer union' includes eventually being a member of the euro as is made clear to all new EU members. Here we reiterate the key findings to illustrate the general problems faced by all euro-zone members who relinquish their own currency. For the UK, with about equal trade with euro and dollar-based trading partners, the micro-economic gains of reduced currency uncertainty failed to occur because zero euro uncertainty is offset by much higher uncertainty against the dollar, the euro being notoriously unstable against the dollar. For many euro-zone countries this is less compelling because they trade more with the euro-zone, but the micro-economic gains are still diluted by it.

Whatever the micro-economics, the macro-economics of losing one's currency were found to be devastating for the UK. Given the shocks of the 1980s and 1990s for which the studies were done, roughly a doubling of the economy's fluctuations was envisaged. Had the shocks that caused the Great Recession been factored in, no doubt the figure would have been much larger.

The truth of such calculations can be seen informally by contrasting the

UK's recovery since the banking crisis with the total failure of recovery of the euro-zone. Comparisons are complicated by the different factors at work in the two regions. The UK's banking system was directly affected much more by the banking crisis – indeed euro-zone banks were only slightly involved in the sub-prime and Lehman crisis, being much less 'global' in general. Indeed initially euro-zone officials were congratulating themselves on avoiding the crisis during 2007–2008 by not having 'Anglo-Saxon' banks. However, the euro-zone was hit by the world contraction post-Lehman and this is the key parallel with the UK. Whereas the UK managed to cut interest rates sharply at end 2008 and the pound dropped sharply as a result, none of the euro-zone's southern countries hit by the euro crisis of rising deficits and government-bond speculation was able to force their currencies down. Their economies collapsed and still have not recovered, taking the euro-zone with them. The UK, however, has been able to recover in spite of the weakness of its major euro-zone trading partner.

Thus we see here the key mistake made by the European elite in embracing the euro in the wake of the Kohl–Mitterrand pact. The euro-zone is now in a state of persistent stagnation, deflation or even worse, essentially because of the removal of national adjustment permitted by exchange rate movement and the failure to replace it with the adjustment mechanisms present in a unified state (such as national fiscal support and benefit systems).

It may be argued that such macro-economic influences – whether from the exchange rate or fiscal policies – will only be temporary because 'supply-side' factors dominate the economy in the medium run. This is certainly true. But a lot of work has found that, through the workings of political economy, failure on economic stability undermines supply-side reform. When matters are going badly, people resist reform measures, which inevitably hits some groups hard: reform always creates losers as well as (more) winners but the problem is that the losers shout louder because they are typically more concentrated, can see the threat and are thus strongly motivated to lobby, whereas the winners are typically dispersed and may not be aware of their upcoming gains.

Those who like a visible current example can look at Japan. In 1989 the Bank of Japan took action to 'burst the bubble' of rising Japanese stock and land prices. Japan has barely grown since: banking problems, deflation and a high yen have dampened any ardour for reform and productivity growth. Even after Mr Abe's recent 'three arrows', it is proving hard against this entrenched mind-set to get his third arrow (of supply-side reform) to fly.

In summary, the EU took a serious wrong turning in 1999 by launching the euro. This tragic mistake looks set to dog the EU's economic future for another decade at least. Sadly it must be a major element in the UK's attitude to continuing membership of the EU.

3.2 SHOULD BRITAIN JOIN THE EURO? THE COSTS AND BENEFITS[1]

During the 1980s the issue of Britain's membership of the European Monetary System's Exchange Rate Mechanism (ERM) was a constant source of political controversy, ultimately playing a part in the schism between Margaret Thatcher and her Chancellor, Nigel Lawson, and also in the final drama of her resignation as a serving Prime Minister. As is well-known, Britain entered the ERM in 1990, only to exit from it in 1992. During the 1990s the equivalent monetary issue concerning European exchange rate arrangements was that of joining the euro. After the ERM's travails in the early 1990s the leaders of continental European countries, notably Chancellor Kohl of Germany and President Mitterrand of France, decided to embark on monetary union. In the Maastricht Treaty Britain negotiated an opt-out from this. In January 1999 the euro was launched as a virtual currency (that is, for banking transactions) and in January 2002 the euro materialized as a transactions currency, with notes and coins. The debate in Britain was focused by the knowledge that joining the euro is in large measure irreversible, unlike joining the ERM. It is of course not impossible to leave the euro; anything in politics is possible. But joining does put enormous barriers in the way of leaving: for example there is no provision in the Rome Treaty (as subsequently amended, notably by the Maastricht Treaty) for doing so and therefore it would involve a violation of the treaty, with unpredictable ramifications. The question of joining was therefore considered of such importance, both practical and constitutional, that it forced politicians to offer the people a referendum. The Blair government stated that if and when it decided to recommend joining, it would then hold a binding referendum on entry. It also let it be known that its decisions would be highly dependent on the economics of joining; it admitted that there were political and constitutional considerations but suggested that these were secondary. The Chancellor of the Exchequer drew up the Five Economic Tests for entry with the full authority of the government; it was said that they must be met 'clearly and unambiguously'.

In brief (for a full list see Bush, 2001, p. 27), the first test concerned whether the UK had achieved 'convergence' with the rest of the EU; the second whether there was sufficient economic flexibility in the UK and the EU to avoid problems; the third concerned the effects on inward investment; the fourth concerned the effects on the City of London. In a fit of common sense, the Chancellor and his economic advisers listed as the 'fifth test' for Britain's entry into the euro the general economic effects of monetary union on the British economy, thus in effect sweeping all the other tests up into this very one. This provided a welcome opportunity to consider the overall economic calculus of entry.

Before we begin this calculus we should mention politics, however. The difficulty of placing economics at the centre of the decision was a source of continuous tension in the debate, within all the parties. The problem was that the driving force of monetary union on the continent has always been political; it has been seen by most of its protagonists, certainly its original ones, Chancellor Kohl and President Mitterrand, as a measure that would propel participants into political union at a faster pace. Indeed, the economic problems monetary union would throw up were regarded by them as a useful extra propellant. This has meant that these continental leaders have constantly applied pressure on the UK to join for the same political reasons – they want us to join the club they have in mind, in order to enjoy our assistance (our strengths) and to limit our ability to compete with it and even undermine it by doing things differently. But within the UK there are many, including a large majority of the public, who do not share this continental vision of ultimate political union; they want Britain to be an independent nation in a Europe of independent but cooperating nations. As a result, those UK politicians who want Britain to join the euro have couched the case in economic terms, to avoid alienating this majority opinion; they have generally argued that it will not lead to political union and that those continental politicians wanting such a union are in retreat. Those UK politicians who oppose UK entry have felt no such necessity to downplay the political risks of submergence in a European superstate. Like most serious political arguments, there is little chance that either side will be convinced by evidence or reasoned debate to change their position.

It is against this background that we consider the economic costs and benefits. Fortunately, economics has developed fairly robust means of testing arguments and evidence. There is a body of economic theory within which the logic of arguments can be evaluated. Furthermore we have increasingly good access to data and econometric tools, so that evidence can be brought to bear. This means that, much as some participants in the debate would like the economics to be vague and impressionistic so that political preferences could easily be dressed up as economic arguments, modern economics does not easily oblige.

Our aim is to set out in as clear a way as we can what the economic arguments on both sides are, and then to discuss what theory and evidence we can bring to bear on them so as to evaluate the gains and losses to the

UK economy were it to join. Economics is a quantitative subject; therefore what is true for the UK may not be true for other countries. We will see that there are both gains and losses. For the UK the calculation will depend on its particular characteristics. For other countries with other characteristics the calculation may well therefore be different. But, needless to say, this chapter is about the UK only.

3.3   THE BENEFITS OF JOINING THE EURO

The economic benefits put forward for the euro consist of three main elements: the reduction in the 'transactions costs' of changing currency; the reduction of exchange risk leading to greater trade and foreign investment with the rest of Europe, and to a lower risk-premium embodied in the cost of raising capital; and increased transparency in price comparison.

Transactions Costs

Being in the euro would mean that currency exchange between pounds and euros would no longer occur; this would save resources (reflected in the margins of currency dealers in a competitive market). The EU Commission did a study (EC, 1990) of the savings and found that on average across the euro members there would be savings in dealers' margins of 0.4 per cent of GDP. However, for countries with advanced banking systems, such as the UK, it found the saving to be much smaller, at around 0.1 per cent of GDP. The reason was that the vast proportion of currency exchanges between pounds and euros take place via the banking system (as for example in inter-firm trade payments or credit card payments). These transactions, whatever margins may be marked up on them, are costless in resources since in a computerized banking transaction conversion of a payment into another currency requires the computer merely to perform one extra operation, at essentially zero marginal cost. So the cost only arises when people change currency hand-to-hand, basically small tourist transactions.

At the time 0.1 per cent of UK GDP was about £1 billion per year, a fairly small sum though of course it is a gain that in principle continues indefinitely, at a level depending on the share of such currency exchanges in GDP. It seems rather likely in fact that these exchanges will steadily diminish in importance as credit card and other banking payment mechanisms penetrate ever deeper into tourist practice. A reasonable practical assumption might be that it would remain about constant in absolute terms at £1 billion in 2000 prices.

The transactions cost argument does not end there. In order to join the

euro there must be a large one-off transactions cost in the form of changing the pound into euros, including changing over the vending machines,
the accounting systems and the banks' high street machines. There were a
range of estimates of this, which were usefully reviewed by the House of
Commons Trade and Industry Committee (House of Commons, 2000),
together with work of their own. They concluded that a reasonable central
estimate of the changeover cost was £30 billion.

To reach an overall assessment of the net transactions cost one must
either turn this last one-off cost into an annual charge or convert the
ongoing gain above into a 'present value equivalent'. This is easily done.
If we take the real rate of interest as around 4 per cent, then the annual-
ized charge on £30 billion is £1.2 billion, slightly more than the £1 billion
annual gain. Or equivalently the present value of £1 billion is £25 billion
(£1 billion/0.04), rather less than the one-off cost. By playing with the real
rate assumed, one can push the comparison either way, and in any case
both sets of estimates must be regarded as of doubtful accuracy. In other
words, the transactions cost argument for going in turns out to be on
balance of little weight.

Exchange Risk, Trade, Foreign Investment and the Cost of Capital

The core of the argument for going into the euro is the elimination of
exchange risk against the euro. It is argued (for example, in Britain in
Europe, 2000) that this elimination is like the removal of a trade barrier
and will promote much more trade with Europe, will increase foreign
investment in the UK, and will reduce the cost of capital by merging the
rather risky and limited sterling capital market into the bigger and less
risky euro capital market.

Let us examine this argument in two stages. First, let us assume that
exchange risk is an important influence on trade, foreign investment and
the cost of capital. Second, we will consider this assumption critically.

So, assuming exchange risk is a big factor, consider whether joining the
euro will actually reduce it or not and, if so, by how much. Here we immediately trip over the key point that to join the euro is not to join a world
currency but a regional one. Unfortunately for our exchange risk we trade
very heavily with the dollar area. Let us not get tied up in the vexed question of the exact shares of our trade with Europe and with the USA, and
what sorts of trade should be counted (in goods? in goods and services?
or in all cross-border transactions including foreign investment and earn-
ings on them?). The point is that if we regard exchange risk as a sort of
tax on transactions involving exchanging currency, then it is plain that
the broadest definition should be used for the 'trade' affected by this tax.

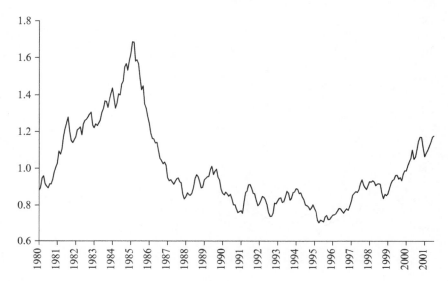

Figure 3.1   Euro per US dollar, 1980–2001

Most of the world outside Europe either uses the dollar or is tied to it in some formal or informal way. We might then say, in a rough and ready way, that we trade and invest half with the euro area and half with the dollar area. (This, by the way, is not the same issue as the currency in which trade is denominated or invoiced, in which the dollar heavily preponderates; invoicing is about how the risk is shared between buyers and sellers, not about the total risk involved.)

It so happens that the euro/dollar exchange rate has been highly variable for a very long time: see Figure 3.1, which shows the DM/dollar rate up to January 1999 and thereafter links on the euro–dollar rate (this linkage assumes that the DM would have been the dominating element in the behaviour of the euro, had it existed before). Nor have the sources of that variability been removed. They include the very different philosophies of regulation ('Rhenish' versus 'Anglo-Saxon' capitalism) which lead to swings in market sentiment about likely future success; differences in business cycle timing which cause swings in interest rates; and differences in adoption of new technologies. It is true that differences in inflation are now small but that has been so now since at least the mid-1980s; this has not stopped very large swings in the exchange rate due to these other reasons which affect the 'real exchange rate' (that is, the exchange rate adjusted for relative inflation.) Figure 3.2 contrasts this experience with the UK's real exchange rate variation over the same period; the

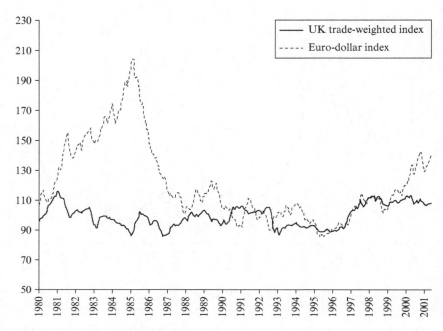

Note: Bank of England 1990 = 100.

Figure 3.2   UK trade-weighted index, 1980–2001

UK has managed to keep these swings moderate and related to its own
business cycle needs.

These graphs show experience up to the euro's creation. It is of interest to compare experience since, particularly as that covers the period
since the euro's creation. Figures 3.3 and 3.4 reveal that the situation
has not altered: the euro has continued to fluctuate sharply against
the dollar, while sterling has moved moderately against the average of
all currencies, essentially as needed for its own problems, notably the
banking crisis when sterling depreciated sharply to offset the recession-
ary consequences.

Notice how the swings of the euro against the dollar since 2000 have
been massive – no less than a halving of the dollar's value per euro and
a recovery since of 50 per cent. Notice also that had the pound been
fixed against the euro in 2000, it would have appreciated against the
dollar by as much as the euro did. Turn now to the actual behaviour of
sterling from 2000: it remained fairly stable against the average of all
currencies until the crisis struck in 2007, when it fell sharply as part of

Note: Bank of England 1990 = 100.

Figure 3.3   UK trade-weighted index, 1990–2014

Figure 3.4   Euro per dollar, 1990–2014

the package of policies designed to counteract recession. Had sterling been in the euro, that would have been impossible since the euro did not depreciate.

The problem then for the UK is that if we join the euro we thereby increase our exchange risk against the dollar as the euro swings around against it. If we remain outside, the pound can as these swings occur 'go between' the two, rather like someone sitting on the middle of a seesaw.

The graph of the UK's exchange rate – Figures 3.2 and 3.3 – juxtaposed against the euro/dollar exchange rate shows rather clearly that we have been able to enjoy less volatility in our overall exchange rate by tying to neither of these two big regional currencies.

We have some concrete experience of experimenting with such tying. When we first shadowed and then tied to the DM from 1988–92, we experienced substantial average exchange rate volatility as German reunification led to a large appreciation of the DM against the dollar. That too can be seen clearly in Figure 3.2. Since we left the ERM in 1992 the DM first continued to appreciate against the dollar and then from 1995 began to plunge; from January 1999 its euro successor has plunged further. The pound has fluctuated less in its average value.

So what we find is that there is no necessary gain in exchange risk reduction in joining the euro and that it is even possible that our overall exchange risk would rise. This message is confirmed by stochastic simulations on the Liverpool Model of the UK, reported in Minford (2001), where we find that the variability of the real exchange rate actually rises slightly in the euro compared with floating. The standard deviation of the UK real exchange rate is just under 11 per cent under floating and just over 11 per cent when in the euro under the standard assumptions we make; under the whole variety of other assumptions that we investigate, this relationship between the two hardly changes, average variability in the euro always being a little bit higher than that under floating. This, perhaps rather surprising finding essentially comes from the very large shocks injected by the variations in the euro's own real exchange rate (basically against the dollar area) into the UK's real exchange rate; in other words, exactly the factor we worry about above, that the euro/dollar rate is highly volatile.

From the viewpoint of UK households' welfare, we must also stress that the composition of currency risk is also a factor. A doubling of dollar risk for the elimination of euro risk would be welfare-reducing, even though this would keep 'average risk' unchanged; the reason is the usual one in economics of 'diminishing marginal utility'. The gains I make as a euro trader get progressively smaller as the risk falls to zero, but the losses made by you as a dollar trader get progressively larger as your risk rises to a doubling. So add up all your losses and they dominate my overall gains from the changeover to the euro. In short, adopting the euro could actually diminish UK welfare as a result of exchange risk both in total and in composition.

Let us now turn to the second leg of the argument and ask just how important exchange risk is as a factor determining trade, foreign investment and the cost of capital – both in general and specifically for the UK. This concerns the extent to which modern financial markets can diversify this risk away; the more they can, the cheaper for example the 'hedging' deal they can offer a trader (that is, a trader who is exposed to foreign exchange risk can insure it by covering his exposed position by buying or selling foreign currency for future delivery from a financier, usually a bank, that then carries the risk). Without going into the rather involved theory, the risk can be diversified away to the extent that a currency gyrates independently of general trends or fluctuations – by pooling a lot of independent risks in a large portfolio a bank can largely eliminate these sources of risk at the portfolio level. On top of this, big enough financial intermediaries can ignore moderate amounts of risk, acting as a 'risk-neutral' insurer.

In trade the main risk is that the exchange rate will change after the deal has been concluded; this will usually be over the short term, say months or a year. In foreign investment the risk is that the plant in the host country will experience a rise in costs of production that is not matched by a fall in the exchange rate. That is, the country's real exchange rate will rise, so reducing real profitability; there is then the further risk that its real exchange rate will fall relative to the investor country's, so causing profits to be worth less on repatriation. In raising capital, the capital provider faces the risk that the loan or share will be devalued by an exchange rate fall. In each case the risk involving the exchange rate is slightly different but in all cases the question is the same: can financial markets diversify away this risk to a level sufficient to ignore? The broad answer will be that if a country's exchange rate or real exchange rate largely varies with domestic factors which are therefore idiosyncratic, then its exchange risk will be highly diversifiable. To the extent to which a country is highly vulnerable to world or general turbulence, it is not. One can see therefore that a country that is well-run, with a sound monetary policy and a flexible supply side, should be able to withstand general turbulence; it will have its own upsets of course but these can be diversified against by the international financial community by investing in foreign assets with which these domestic shocks are uncorrelated.

We may then turn to the question of whether exchange risk will affect a country's domestic real interest rate. The theory tells us that through the international movement of funds to take advantage of arbitrage and speculative opportunities domestic real interest rates will be equal to the 'world' real interest rate (which we can approximate by that of the dollar, the world's dominant currency) plus a risk-premium reflecting the non-diversifiable volatility of the exchange rate. The discussion in the previous paragraph immediately tells us that this risk-premium will be small for a reasonably well-managed economy.

So the theory suggests that a well-managed country should not have much of a problem with exchange risk in general. Its cost of capital will be at world market rates; its foreign investors will be calm about possible future movements in the real exchange rate; and its traders will have a wide scope to hedge at modest cost. On the other hand a badly-managed country vulnerable to crises triggered by world recession, for example, because of poor monetary policy and inflexible labour markets could well find exchange risk a big problem. Such indeed seems to have been the position of Italy before its accession to the euro was agreed and this accounts for the eagerness with which Italy pursued a campaign to join the euro against German reluctance.

We may at this point address the argument (made much of in Britain in Europe, 2000) that a country's exchange rate is vulnerable to 'bubbles', that is, irrational movements based on pure sentiment rather than fundamentals. The best-managed country can have its exchange rate 'attacked by speculators' in such a bubble and this, it is argued, will generally be triggered by world events in a contagious way so that their possibility cannot easily be diversified against. By joining the euro such bubbles are closed down, it is further argued. However, the evidence for such bubbles is poor and the theory surrounding them is controversial (in *Advanced Macroeconomics: A Primer*, Minford and Peel (2002) review the theory carefully and suggest that in the end it relies on systematic irrationality among market participants). We can furthermore account for what are claimed to be bubbles in terms of natural market concerns about future policies; provided these are stable, exchange rate volatility should be limited. If we look at the data, as in Minford (2001), we find that the volatility in the pound's risk-premium (the supposed source of a bubble in the exchange rate and so the economy) is not an important factor in determining the variability of the economy under floating. When it is tripled, the comparison with being in the euro changes only modestly: the economy remains far more variable in the euro than under floating. So, even if some of the volatility of the UK's risk-premium were due to bubbles, the evidence reveals it as of no practical importance.

There are therefore good theoretical reasons for doubting the importance of exchange risk as a factor affecting the UK; such risk as there is should be readily diversifiable in financial markets, resulting in little cost to insure and so having little impact on the real economy. The empirical studies available tend to support this judgement. A wide range of studies surveyed and in many cases commissioned by the IMF found little, if any, impact of exchange rate volatility on trade (a typical example is Bailey et al., 1987). In a theoretical study of this issue, Bacchetta and van Winkoop (2000) note that 'the substantial empirical literature examining the link between exchange-rate uncertainty and trade has not found a consistent relationship', adding that 'in papers that find a negative relationship, it is generally weak'; the theoretical general equilibrium benchmark model they consider implies no relationship at all between trade and the exchange rate regime.

The factors moving foreign investment have also been widely studied, and foreign exchange risk is generally found to be a minor consideration (evidence bearing on the UK is examined, for example, in Leach, 2001). As for the cost of capital, an exchange risk premium is found for countries that have poor domestic policies; the UK has in the past suffered from this problem – one has only to go back to the battle for reforms in the 1970s and the early 1980s to see this in the data. But in the 1990s, once the exit from the ERM had been digested and a new monetary consensus against inflation forged, we saw the emergence of a minimal risk-premium over world capital costs. For example UK gilts now sell on yield similar to US Treasuries.

We should mention two studies that appear to point the opposite way, both of them cited as important evidence in Britain in Europe (2000). The first, by Professor Andrew Rose of Berkeley (Rose, 1999), finds a statistical relationship between the size of bilateral trade of two countries and whether they are in a monetary union; his coefficient implies that trade is tripled by monetary union. However, economists have been highly sceptical of this claim (see Rose, 1999; also Persson, 2001, and Nitsch, 2001) on the grounds that the coefficient comes from the experience of many small dependent economies in monetary unions with large, usually 'mother', countries; there is really no way of distinguishing the effect of close ties of dependency on close trade patterns from that of monetary union itself. Monetary union is a sign of an extraordinary closeness of relations in general, from which trade closeness is bound to flow. Rose claims he has 'controlled' for such closeness factors by including proxies for these such as 'colonial dependency'. This unfortunately does not resolve the problem; suppose there was a colony that broke its ties with the mother country and as part of that broke up its monetary union. The only distinction between it and another colony that did not would be its absence of monetary union. So monetary union would in effect be the indicator of closeness of general ties. In effect this problem (known as 'selection bias') is insuperable without being able somehow to choose the cases where monetary union did and did not take place randomly, quite separately from the cases where political ties occurred or broke down. If these things occur together, because of some third unobserved cause, then there is no means of distinguishing their effect.

The second study is by John McCallum of the Royal Bank of Canada (McCallum, 1995). It concerns Canada's trade with the US. He shows that in spite of its effectively free market with the USA, Canada trades much less with the USA than it does within its own borders, even in contiguous states. Britain in Europe (2000) claims this as evidence that were Canada to have a monetary union with the USA, trade would be much higher. Yet the McCallum paper claims nothing of the sort, merely that 'the existence of the border' reduces trade; indeed the paper makes no mention of monetary union. Canada, being a different country, has a myriad of different institutions that between them change incentives to trade, these being summarized in 'the border'. One of them plainly is a different currency but it is only one of many. As with Rose's study it is impossible to divorce the closeness of ties evidenced by monetary union from the effects of these ties themselves; were Canada to be in a monetary union with the US it would no doubt be because there was a high degree of mutual trust and a willingness to remove institutional differences. Their removal would lead to a Canadian province on one side of the US border being essentially like a US state on the other side – regulatory arrangements, legal procedures and so on would be the same, there would be no customs posts or different forms to fill in and so on. 'The border' would have gone in total – not just the separate currencies.

Unfortunately, to determine the separate effect of monetary union requires that monetary union be something that can be varied quite separately from general closeness, as argued above; and the data do not provide this experiment. These two studies, in spite of their sophisticated econometrics, do not get around this problem in the case of monetary union. We can look at the evidence of the effects on trade of exchange rate volatility; there at least one can find separate movement of the volatility measure divorced from the movement of other factors. As we have seen, it does not reveal much, if any, effect.

There are a few cases where countries have maintained normal relations in other respects but have decided to make or break monetary unions. Flandreau (2001) examined the cases of the Latin Monetary Union of 1865 (between Belgium, France, Italy and Switzerland) and the Scandinavian Monetary Union of 1873 (between Sweden, Denmark and Norway) and found no evidence of trade effects of monetary union. Aristotelous (2001) found none on US–UK trade from movements on and off the Gold Standard and the break-up of Bretton Woods. Most relevantly, for the UK, Thom and Walsh (2002) found no trade effects from Ireland's breaking-up of monetary union with the UK in 1979. What all these studies confirm is that trade patterns are determined by comparative advantage, not by monetary factors, not even monetary union. If monetary risk is like a trade barrier, then it is – as we might have suspected from the theory of diversifiability – an exiguously small one.

In conclusion, this, the major argument adduced for entry, does not appear to be of much quantitative significance. It might even go the wrong way. One can agree that having a common money across the world would bring some gains of market integration – even if modest – while disagreeing that adopting a regional currency like the euro will bring even modest gains.

Transparency of Price Comparison

Prices, it is said, will be easier to compare in a foreign currency; hence the consumer will gain from greater competition bringing enhanced price similarity (adjusted for quality differences). For countries with populated land borders such as Belgium or the Netherlands, the argument has some force as border people are constantly involved in price comparisons which could be costly in time. However, the UK has no land borders with the euro-zone (other than the mainly rural one between Northern Ireland and Eire). So the argument in our case can only be of interest for substantial traded goods or services: we are hardly going to be comparing the price of Coca-Colas and haircuts (unlike the residents of Maastricht, say). The main example given is motor cars, where it is argued that UK car prices are higher than on the continent because we have a different currency.

It is quite important to distinguish the argument from those of transactions costs or exchange risk already considered. It is identifying a special transactions cost – namely that of comparing prices which, with different currencies, involves a calculator or some extra mental arithmetic. So in the case of cars it is being claimed that the extra cost of getting out a calculator to compare, say, Belgian prices of Fords with those in Birmingham is an important element keeping up prices in Birmingham. A moment's reflection reveals the absurdity of this claim; assume that there were competitive dealers offering to get you a Belgian car in place of a Birmingham one; would they not first quote you the sterling-equivalent prices or, if not, would you not find it a trivial chore to get out your calculator when making such a big purchase?

In fact there have been a number of investigations (mainly by the Competition Commission and its predecessor body, the Monopolies and Mergers Commission (MMC)) of why car prices are different in the UK from the continent. The major reason (MMC, 1992) found has been the exclusive-dealer system, which permits car companies to prevent cross-trading; another has been different regulatory systems (including driving on the left/right); another has been the tax treatment of company cars and the resulting vigour of the second-hand market. Even the existence of the internet, which could lower the costs of trading, has apparently not much affected the matter; internet traders have just as much difficulty getting around the car companies.

One is driven to conclude that, apart from border towns where obviously comparing small items would be costly in different currencies, this transparency argument is of little interest. As border towns are not relevant to the UK, that ends it from the UK viewpoint.

3.4   THE COSTS OF EMU FOR THE UK

There are three main economic costs that have been identified in joining the euro: the difficulty of dealing with shocks without the use of independent interest rates and exchange rate movements; the effects of 'harmonization' initiatives associated with the euro project (generally known as Economic and Monetary Union, or EMU); and the concerns that we could be involved in the bailing out of continental countries with financial problems, associated particularly with state pension deficits but also, as we have seen, in the euro crisis with general debt problems.

Our focus here is on these economic arguments. But we should point out in passing that the nature of the political union implicit in the monetary union plans is relevant to the last two economic arguments. Both harmonization and bail-out concerns are directly related to the strength of the desire for political union. The stronger the push for political union the more of a constituency there is for harmonization as well as for mutual cross-country support. Britain in Europe (2000) argues that harmonization is a strictly separate matter from the euro project and that bail-out is explicitly ruled out by the Maastricht Treaty. This, however, fails to recognize the way that EU institutions have been deliberately used to advance the cause of political union, for example: the expectation of the European Court that its judgements should advance unification; the use of the Single Market Act with its qualified majority voting to force the limitation of working hours on the UK as a health and safety measure; the series of summits organized by the Commission under successive country presidencies to further union in foreign and defence policy; and finally of course the massive bail-outs organized in response to the euro-zone crisis. EMU, the euro project, creates a further set of institutions through which arrangements can be made to increase unification between EMU members; linkages can be set up that get around national 'separateness' or the vetoing of bail-out – 'support' after all can be 'voluntary' or 'common taxes' can be 'redistributed'. Joining EMU means that the UK is subject to its extra set of arrangements. It is like being caught in a double spider's web when you are lightly entangled in a single one from which you can still disentangle yourself.

In effect EMU is a process which is designed to produce a high degree of economic and political integration. In joining it, a country is unable to avoid signing up to that process; staying outside, it can remain part of the existing treaty which deals with trade, movements of productive factors and the Single Market. Clearly, an EMU which was a system designed solely to share a common money, with member countries remaining independent countries, cooperating merely in the enforcement of good competitive norms and the freest possible trade would be a different proposition and the arguments that follow would need important modification. Indeed were the EU and its EMU branch to be intended as a sort of early twentieth-century Gold Standard world writ large, with free trade, untrammelled labour mobility, competition and flexible labour markets, it would offer some definite attractions to be put in the balance (and clearly affecting the balance of arguments on the five tests). However, it is plain to see that this is not the EMU on offer. The EMU we are assessing here is the one that is on offer.

Shocks Without an Independent Currency

A single currency implies a single interest rate unless there are such barriers to the movement of money as exchange controls or differential taxes on interest rates – all of which are of course explicitly forbidden under the Maastricht Treaty, with no conceivable loophole.

One can understand this point by considering whether York and Manchester could have different deposit rates or lending rates. If, for example, York paid higher deposit rates and charged higher loan rates, then all the deposits would flow to York and all the borrowing would flow to Manchester. Both sets of banks would go bankrupt in a matter of weeks; York with no lending business, Manchester with no deposits. So of course they must push their rates into line to stop these ('arbitrage') flows of business.

This could be prevented by exchange controls stopping people moving their money or their loan business. Or else York could have a separate exchange rate. Plainly by joining the UK monetary union, they give up their separate exchange rate and having no powers to levy controls they therefore share an interest rate. This then happens inside the euro between London and Frankfurt. It is worth dwelling on this since some people ask why there cannot be different interest rates for different regions or industries within a union; why all the fuss, they ask. The answer is there could be, but only with regional exchange controls, which would be very bad for any economy, besides being unlawful.

At the heart of the case against joining the euro is the consequence of abandoning a separate interest rate for the UK, which comes with a separate exchange rate or currency. In effect the exchange rate, by moving, allows one country's interest rate to be different from another's. It is sometimes said that 'in a globalized world' a country cannot really have an independent monetary policy, that is, a different interest rate that it chooses. This is simply wrong. The way monetary policy works is precisely that it engineers an interest rate to suit its own conditions and objectives and that the exchange rate moves ('floats') to prevent money flowing in or out of the rest of the world to frustrate that chosen interest rate. It does so because under floating exchange rates, as normally defined, the country's central bank does not intervene in the foreign exchange market; if it were to do so, it would compromise its ability to set its own interest rates because by exchanging its own money for foreign money it would alter its domestic money market conditions and so its interest rates.

For example, suppose Japan lowers interest rates; holders of yen deposits then have an incentive to move their money to London, say, or New York to get the higher interest rates there. But as they do so they find that they cannot go to the Bank of Japan, the central bank, and get dollars or pounds because the BOJ will not want to take in the yen in exchange as that would reduce the yen money supply and raise interest rates back up again with the shortage of money. So those who want to move their money have to find someone in the private market to buy the dollars or pounds from. As all these extra yen are offered on the market for pounds and dollars, they drive down the yen; as people holding dollars or pounds do not want to sell them, the yen goes down until the market is in equilibrium. This equilibrium will happen when the yen is so low that it is expected to go up again; then the expected capital gain on a rising yen will just offset the much lower interest rate on yen deposits. Of course when that happens, those Japanese who wanted to move their money out will no longer want to do so; so in effect they will happily keep their money on deposit at the lower Japanese interest rate. In short, the exchange rate moves to 'insulate' the home interest rate chosen from whatever interest rates prevail abroad; movements of money do not frustrate the chosen interest rate because the exchange rate moves enough to stop the money from actually moving.

What this means is that with a separate currency which freely floats as required by differing interest rates or other factors that influence people's desires to put money in different countries, the Bank of England has the power to alter interest rates to suit the UK. The exchange rate will then move as necessary to permit this. Joining the euro means that the UK interest rate is set by the European Central Bank in Frankfurt to suit, in its chosen sense, the needs of the whole euro-zone, which may of course be very different from the UK's. For example, as we found when in the Exchange Rate Mechanism (which imposed fixed exchange rates though stopped short of creating a common currency), if the UK is in recession and the rest of the euro-zone is not, then its recession can become longer and worse because interest rates cannot be lowered. With repeated differential shocks this would mean that the UK would suffer greater variability of unemployment, output and prices than it would with freedom to set its own interest rates.

It is theoretically possible that having the same interest rate as the rest of the euro-zone would not cause this higher UK variability – or at least not much. These conditions are known as the 'optimal currency area' conditions:

1. Shocks could be very similar in effect: 'symmetric'. This might be because industries are similar; because the economy has a similar structure of financial and other arrangements so that it responds in the same way to similar shocks; or because it has a similar trade pattern and, even better, trades almost exclusively with other euro-zone countries.
2. There are powerful fiscal compensation mechanisms, as happens in most countries: a region hit by a shock benefits from paying fewer taxes, gets more benefit payments, and may get special regional assistance.
3. Labour moves freely so that a region doing well sucks in workers unemployed in regions doing badly; this happens to a great extent in the USA.
4. Wages are highly flexible so that a region hit by a nasty shock causing unemployment lowers its wages and prices, while other regions raise theirs; this then quickly sets in train a counteracting creation of employment in the former and contraction of it in the latter.

These conditions are effectively what the Chancellor's tests 1 and 2 are concerned with. Casual, as well as detailed, observation reveals that conditions 1–4 are not met in the euro-zone (for an exhaustive treatment see Bush, 2001).

On condition 1, evidence of business cycle behaviour suggests that the UK cycle has been far closer to the US one than to the European one. The UK's response to interest rate movements is also differentially responsive owing to the preponderance of variable-rate mortgages.

On condition 2, plainly the EU essentially has no budget for such purposes. On condition 3, language, differential national regulations and housing market rigidities make mobility difficult except for certain types of low-skilled worker (such as hotel and catering staff).

As for condition 4, in the UK there is nowadays a reasonable degree of wage flexibility as a result of the substantial liberalizing reforms of the last two decades. But there is little in the rest of the euro-zone where strong unions and heavy regulation on working conditions make it difficult; the main hope would be that unions are willing in time to negotiate wage moderation, which in certain circumstances could be a weak substitute for flexibility. However, this may take a long time and substantial unemployment to achieve, so it is unlikely to avoid substantial unemployment variability.

Hence the evidence is in a general way suggestive that conditions 1–4 will not be of much help to the UK. However counter-claims are made and in the end it is an empirical matter, to be assessed in the light of evidence on the UK's likely behaviour in the face of likely shocks. It is this that is addressed in Minford (2001). The method (known as 'stochastic simulation') is described in detail there. In short, it is to pepper a well-tried model of the UK with a large number of typical shocks drawn from past experience; and then to see what the variability of the economy is under the two alternative monetary regimes – the euro regime versus policy as now set by the Bank of England under floating exchange rates.

We can summarize these findings as follows. Joining the euro would increase the variability of the UK economy – the 'boom-and-bust' factor – by about 75 per cent. This is also a widely-used measure of the cost involved, as experienced by politicians facing popular pressures. This increased cost is largely insensitive to the sort of ameliorative changes that euro advocates have put forward. Greater UK labour market flexibility helps a bit; so does smaller UK responsiveness to interest rates. But the extent is small; the big difference remains. The reason is that the UK is both unable to respond to shocks optimally with its own interest rate and also is destabilized by euro shocks (especially against the dollar), given that we trade so heavily with the rest of the world. This is the case even though we freely allow fiscal stabilizers full play, not merely the automatic ones but also extra discretionary public spending response to the cycle. Were unemployment to reach the double-digit rates we saw in the early 1980s and early 1990s, the difference of variability would be even larger, and it would be more serious too, as the absolute variation in unemployment would rise more than proportionately with this higher baseline unemployment. Euro advocates claim that outside the euro the pound would suffer enhanced volatility; our estimates allow for the volatility in the pound's risk-premium experienced in the past decade but we checked what would happen to the comparison if we allowed for a tripling of it. Again, the difference is reduced but not much, basically because the economy's built-in monetary shock absorbers work pretty well. That then remains the key point; running a modern economy with popular consent requires efficient shock absorbers, and joining the euro not merely removes them but provides an additional source of shocks from the euro itself.

An earlier study by Barrell and Dury (2000), using the National Institute's multi-country model, found that the costs would be less than ours. If we translate their findings into the terms of our boom and bust index, their index would be 42 per cent higher under the euro than under floating (against our 75 per cent). They find that under the euro UK output (and so by implication unemployment) would be 51 per cent more volatile as measured by its variance against our 27 per cent; this greater effect is probably the result of their model structure being more Keynesian (with less price/wage flexibility). However, on inflation they find rather strangely that inflation volatility would actually fall 44 per cent under the euro – our finding was that it would rise by a massive 880 per cent, essentially because the euro's volatility against the dollar would move traded goods prices around sharply, rather as has happened in Ireland at the start of the euro. On inspection we can account for this different finding in terms of three major differences in the methods they use. First, they assume that the risk-premium on sterling is given by the 'forecasting error' between the forward rate and the exchange rate outturn. However, the two things are different; the risk-premium is an element included in the forward rate as the price of risk, whereas the forecast error is an element occurring later after the price has been quoted. Plainly, the price of risk reflects the anticipation of possible future errors on average (typically their variance); it cannot be assumed to be equal to any and every actual future error. To assume it in a stochastic simulation exercise like this one will in practice make the assumed risk-premium excessively volatile by a large margin.

Second, they assume that UK monetary policy is set according to somewhat arbitrary rules – they impose a rigid postulated 'inflation target' operating rule. We assume, by contrast, that UK interest rates are set according to the rule under which the Monetary Policy Committee (MPC) does the best possible job it can within the freedom given it by floating exchange rates; this involves interest rates reacting to inflation with a weight of 1.5 against one on output of 0.5, rather similar to what we observe the MPC does in practice. Given that the MPC did a rather good job of stabilizing both inflation and output in an essentially pragmatic way, at least until the banking crisis, and can presumably learn to adjust to changes both in circumstances and the UK's economic behaviour, the Barrell/Dury assumption puts the floating regime under an unfair handicap.

Third, the period from which they draw the shocks with which their model is peppered is 1991–97 during which the crucial euro–dollar exchange rate happens to have been more stable than in the fuller 1986–2000 period we use. One can understand this point more clearly by reference to Figure 3.1 above; there one can see that from 1986 to 1991 the dollar fell considerably against the euro; from 1991–97 it moved up and down moderately; before then rising again in the period to 2000. Thus by omitting both the earlier and the later period, the euro–dollar rate's insta- bility is markedly understated. It is likely that were the Barrell/Dury study to be rerun on this basis, they too would find that inflation volatility would increase under the euro quite substantially. If so, their overall boom-and- bust index would be comparable to ours, thus joining a series of studies of models indicating that this cost would be substantial.

In a recent article Barrell (2002) criticized the Minford study on a number of grounds. The first is that it drew shocks from the 1980s 'for a currency that nobody then assumed would exist'. However, we have to have a sample of shocks for a duration long enough to represent the range of experience the UK might face. The 1991–97 period, chosen by Barrell and Dury, has the problems we saw above; yet even then the euro did not exist. Given the existence of active exchange rate coordination by France (as well as most other countries later forming the euro-zone) with the DM during the 1980s, it seems reasonable to assume that, had the euro existed, it would have behaved something like the average of the euro currencies. As it happens its behaviour from 1997 to 2000 echoed the volatility of the late 1980s as explained already; it would seem safer, given that we must factor in the euro's behaviour, to use a longer period rather than focusing on an artificially less volatile, shorter period.

Secondly, Barrell argues that it neglects the reaction of the ECB through its interest-rate setting to the euro's behaviour and in general to UK shocks which are correlated with euro-zone shocks. However, Minford allowed fully for any correlation between the euro interest rate and both the euro and all UK shocks; the drawings of shocks made for the stochastic simu- lation were done by the vector bootstrap method in which the whole set of shocks for a quarter is drawn at once. This means that the correlations between the shocks in the data are fully preserved in the simulations. Hence we are allowing fully for the historical reaction of euro-zone interest rates to UK and euro shocks. Barrell asserts that this can be done better by simulating a multi-country model in which an assumption is made about the ECB's reaction function. But this would be to substitute assumptions for actual historical reactions.

On the particular point that UK inflation volatility would be greater inside the euro, Barrell counters that the ECB would react to dampen it down (unlike in the case of Ireland). Would it do so more than by the average of euro-zone behaviour already captured in the historical correla- tions? One must doubt it, given that the UK would be one country of 13, with a GDP weight of about a fifth.

Interestingly, when all is said and done, Barrell and Dury find a much greater increase of UK output volatility on going into the euro than Minford does. It is over inflation that they differ, and there it is hard to resist the conclusion that they have made a variety of special assumptions that have the effect of greatly understating the inflationary problems the UK would experience, along the lines that Ireland so dramatically found on entering the euro.

Harmonization

As we saw above, what is needed to make EMU work better – that is, to avoid undue instability in the economy as a result of losing control of monetary policy – is greater wage flexibility, in the absence of the large federal budgets and the labour mobility that the EU does not have. However, there is little sign of the emergence of this flexibility. Instead, it is being suggested on the continent that what is needed is 'harmonization' of taxes and other institutions. The argument appears to be that this will reduce the extent of differences in response to shocks and even increase the similarity of shocks by somehow creating a similarity of industrial structure. The basis for such arguments is extremely tenuous; possibly responses to shocks could become marginally more similar but even this is not clear since the dissimilarities could have been partially offsetting, and certainly there is no reason to suppose it would create a similarity of struc-ture. More seriously, what protagonists of harmonization probably have in mind is the aim of building up central federal institutions which would ultimately have revenues and the power, like any state, to make transfers to and from regions with asymmetric shocks; harmonization does not in itself provide any help for EMU but it is a stepping stone to state powers which would.

Given the preferences of the majority of states in the euro-zone, this harmonization would be around a rate of taxation, social support and regulation well above that currently prevailing in the UK. It is a matter of speculation what exact level of harmonization would be aimed at, but we have calculated the effects of different levels of labour market intervention within the Liverpool Model to illustrate the problem for the UK of finding itself pressured one way or another into adopting such levels. We reviewed these costs earlier in Chapter 3 and do not reproduce them here. The essential point is that joining the euro increases the pressure to adopt such intrusive measures and hence pushes their cost towards the upper limits of those shown in our calculations.

It can be seen that these are large costs, even in the least-cost scenario with its cost at 9 per cent of GDP and 10 per cent on unemployment. The high-cost scenario is obviously hugely damaging, at 20 per cent of GDP and an unquantifiable rise in unemployment.

These are just illustrations, a sample of effects. Damage would similarly be done by the forced raising of tax rates – as yet less likely, but only in the short term.

Some of these changes are coming in to a certain extent as a result of EU pressures independent of EMU. However, harmonization is part of the centralizing EMU agenda; and the club within a club that meets to decide policy on EMU matters will increase the pressure to move this agenda forwards for members of the euro-zone. Joining EMU would put increased impetus behind the harmonization agenda for the UK.

3.5   THE BAIL-OUT ISSUE AND THE ROLE OF EMU

Bail-out, the Euro-zone Crisis and the Emerging State Pension Crisis

The three largest nations in the euro-zone, Germany, France and Italy, had serious projected state pension deficits as evaluated in 1996 by an OECD paper (Roseveare et al., 1996), which projected them to reach respectively about 10 per cent, 8 per cent and 11 per cent of GDP by 2030. Since then Germany, France and Italy have taken some steps to reduce their prospective deficits, but the steps are small. The OECD work has not been updated but various factors have become worse since that study and they may have wiped out the contribution of those policy changes. Notably unemployment is turning out worse and growth slower than expected, especially since the euro-zone crisis struck. Furthermore, euro-zone countries' debt ratios to GDP have risen markedly in recent years under the impact of the crisis and the policies taken in response.

The politics of cutting pension benefits is speculative given that ageing populations will increasingly be dominated by older voters; yet the effects of raising taxation further would be still lower growth and worse unemployment. Hence it must be a matter of concern to the UK that the cost of meeting potentially explosive state financial liabilities might somehow fall in part on the British taxpayer. This is quite over and above the costs of any ordinary bail-out of future debt problems emerging from the current (or some future) crisis. The more integrated EMU becomes, the greater both the political pressures for concerted action and the economic fall-out from letting a fellow-EMU member-state default partially on its debts. This fall-out includes the risk of contamination of one's own debt status as well as indirect losses of trade, public procurement business and any other joint activities.

For just the same reason – fear of bail-out, in their case focused on Italy – German leaders insisted on the Stability and Growth Pact, which is intended to limit state deficits to 1 per cent of GDP other than in exceptional circumstances. The pact creates difficulties for countries wishing to use fiscal policy to stabilize their economies; it even forces countries to override the automatic fiscal stabilizers that come about from the normal fall in tax revenues and rise in benefits as the economy goes into recession. This is because the 1 per cent is not adjusted for the business cycle (such was the German fear that countries would get around it). Discretionary fiscal policy – that is, that deliberately alters tax rates or spending programmes – is probably not an effective stabilizing instrument, being both slow and potentially counter-productive (as Japanese experience illustrates) since rising debt induces households to save more. But to override the automatic stabilizers (which are built into, for example, our simulations in the section above) could certainly worsen cyclical swings. As it happens, the Stability and Growth Pact was first ignored by Germany in the 2000s when it had its own fiscal problems; since the euro-zone crisis, however, it has been reinstated and reinforced.

Yet while it hobbles the fiscal stabilizers, it seems unlikely that the pact would actually stop a serious bail-out problem. Indeed we have seen as much in the context of the euro-zone crisis. State pension liabilities are routinely treated as an off-budget item (that is, pensions are only counted when they are actually paid and the obligation to pay them is not considered as equivalent to a debt); the resulting liabilities can be allowed to run up, threatening prospective deficits, which are ignored until too late. If a country had high unemployment, a recession and political problems, one can easily imagine a sympathetic attitude developing among EMU members to a permissive policy.

It is worth recalling that the prospective state pension deficits of the big three EMU members in 2030 quoted above are projected as equal to over one third of the UK's GDP – that is, nearly as much as the existing 40 per cent tax share of GDP. The risk of even part of this winding up as a charge on the UK taxpayer is a serious worry about entering EMU in an EU of ever-closer union.

Since this was originally written in 2002, bail-outs have occurred on a massive scale for fiscal deficits that have little to do with pensions but that were brought on by the Great Recession. This highlights the way in which the 'ruling out' of bail-out in the Maastricht Treaty has been widely contradicted in practice; indeed, as we have seen, the Stability and Growth Pact was jettisoned in the 2000s, before the banking crisis, in response to requests from Germany itself. It now appears that ever-closer union implies the principle of pan-EU solidarity and with it shared responsibility for the fiscal problems of other EU countries. This will bring with it a large scope for future bail-outs.

3.6   OVERALL CONCLUSIONS

We examined the alleged benefits of joining the euro and found that:

1. The reduction of transactions costs of currency exchange would be small and would be roughly offset by the one-off cost of currency conversion.
2. There would be some gain from eliminating exchange risk against the euro but this could well be largely, or even more than, offset by increased volatility against the dollar with around half our trade broadly defined with countries either on or closely linked to the dollar.
3. We also found that in any case exchange risk does not appear to have an important effect on trade or foreign investment, and in the UK case, on the cost of capital.
4. There are potential benefits from increased price transparency in border areas but this is of no real relevance to the UK; for large traded items this transparency would amount to the trivial saving on use of a calculator.

We then looked at the potential costs of the euro project, or EMU, as it is currently planned, namely a centralizing one with the aim of strengthening political union, and we found that:

1. The loss of independent monetary policy (interest-rate-setting powers) on joining EMU would raise the economy's cyclical instability substantially.
2. The harmonization agenda, motivated by the centralizing aim, could inflict serious damage on UK employment and output by reducing labour competitiveness.
3. There is a risk, in the emerging state pension crisis of the three major EMU members, that under a centralized EMU subject to an ongoing euro-zone crisis, UK taxpayers could find themselves contributing not merely to bail-out funds for a further or extended euro-zone crisis but also to others' state pension deficits, which could by 2030 be worth more than one third of the UK's GDP.

We have considered the political aspects of the euro project only in terms of their relevance to these economic issues (though clearly they are of the utmost importance in the wide public debate). This relevance lies in the political aims of the project which are to centralize power in a political federal union, without abandoning the main social democratic tenets of the major states such as France and Germany that currently dominate the euro membership. It is these aims that dictate the harmonization agenda and these tenets that explain the slowness and unwillingness to cut pension entitlements as a way of curing pension deficits.

Plainly it would be welcome if these political aspects were replaced by a free market approach within a treaty of cooperating nation-states; this would reduce the costs under conditions 2 and 3 above and if wage flexibility and labour mobility were promoted as part of that approach, it would also reduce the costs under condition 1 above. The increasing competitiveness of the euro-zone under it could also lead to a stronger euro, more stable against the dollar, which would improve the assessment of the benefit under condition 2 above.

Yet we have to assess the euro, EMU, project as it is currently planned by the dominant states within the euro-zone. That is how we have done it, in a spirit of realism and honesty. It would be nice to pretend EMU was something else that we would like better, but it is not and it would be wrong for us to assess it as if it was. One can bear in mind the possibility that it could become a different project, but the likelihood of that possibility is extremely small. The final conclusion must be that EMU, as it is constituted and planned, would be very much against British interests to join.

While we have seen that monetary union has also badly damaged the euro-zone and hence the EU project itself, we must reluctantly concede that the dominant EU elite will ensure the survival of the euro regardless of its cost. The EU's explicit objective of 'ever-closer union', now written into the Lisbon Treaty, also implies that membership of the euro-zone must in time become a requirement of being in the EU. It follows that the costs we have identified in this chapter should be assumed eventually to occur as a result of our continued membership of the EU.

NOTE

1. This chapter is an edited and updated version of Minford (2002).

4.   The cost of EU trade policies for the UK

In Part II of this book we will review rather thoroughly the latest statistics on trade and protection for agriculture, manufacturing and services. In this chapter we attempt to pull the threads together and make an estimate of the overall costs to the UK of the EU's trade arrangements, which can be broadly described as a customs union for manufactures together with an elaborate and expensive system of protection for agriculture. As for services, there is no EU trade policy but merely a continuation of national systems of protection; whether we are in the EU or out of it, this remains the same and so we disregard services in our calculations.

4.1   THE COST OF EU PROTECTION

In this section we use measures of protection based on our findings in these following three chapters to estimate their welfare implications for the UK and for the EU. For this, we use a Computable General Equilibrium, CGE, world model we have built to generate estimates of changes in trade that result from this protection.

As we will see in these later chapters it is difficult to get reliable and up-to-date measures of EU protection because the world is constantly changing. In particular China's trade costs are moving rapidly in response to its own opening up and also its rapid internal growth in wages and living standards. Furthermore we cannot obtain direct measures of Chinese prices; our only price measures come from the OECD and cover only OECD members.

To deal with this complex situation we have decided to use two simplifying devices. First, we gauge the latest trends in protection in agriculture and manufacturing by using available broad measures of protection that we have managed to calculate and updating them according to indicators built up by international bodies. For services, as explained above, we assume no protection because there is no general single market in services and therefore no EU customs union: see Table 4.1 for some indicators of national service barriers.

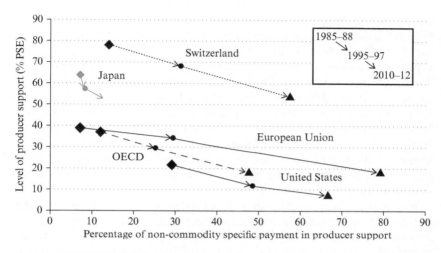

Source: OECD, PSE/CSE database, 2013.

Figure 4.1 Level and composition of producer support for agriculture in OECD countries

Thus for agriculture our estimate of protection is based on Bradford's original tariff-equivalent for 1990 of 36 per cent. OECD estimates of the Producer Subsidy Equivalent within the EU (PSE, a measure of essentially the same protective margin) is approximately the same for this period, as can be seen from Figure 4.1. By 2010–12 their estimate has fallen to around half, at about 18 per cent. We take this latest figure to be approximately the current measure. Plainly change continues as farming adapts; one of the indicators of change is the percentage (shown in the Figure) of non-commodity support in the total, which has by now reached 80 per cent. What this implies is that farmers are in effect being compensated for not growing food on their land. Presumably it is this type of measure that is gradually reducing the PSE; to project where protection may be in 2020, our 'target year' for this calculation, we take it that it will be reduced further in line with this trend. In the spirit of avoiding spurious apparent accuracy we put the measure then at 10 per cent.

If we turn to manufacturing, the situation is more complex still.

It is usually assumed that since the various GATT and WTO rounds have brought manufactured trade tariffs down across the world including the EU, EU protection is light in this sector. However, as Chapter 6 below will show, in the wake of retreating tariffs governments have been given broad discretion to reach agreements on trade quotas, to impose anti-dumping duties or to threaten them and negotiate pre-emptive price rises by importers. Furthermore, these processes reinforce the power of cartels to be established and to survive; thus what starts as temporary protection against 'dumping' ends as the equivalent of a permanent tariff. Tariffs are transparent, but these measures are hard to monitor. While we know how many duties have been imposed and what trade agreements have been made, we cannot easily find out what pre-emptive measures have been taken, nor can we tell whether agreements which have notionally lapsed have done so effectively (especially if a cartel of producers has been implicitly allowed to perpetuate it, as just noted). Calculating the tariff-equivalent has to be done by looking at the price-raising effect of all the various interventions.

Fortunately there are data on prices now on a wide scale owing to the purchasing power parity calculations being done by international organizations. A pioneering study by Bradford of the price differentials between major OECD countries and their least cost OECD supplier suggested that the EU was substantially more protectionist in impact than the USA even though the latter has resorted to a similar number of anti-dumping duties (see Table 4.2). Averaging across the EU countries studied (Germany, Netherlands, Belgium and the UK) Bradford's figures, which are adjusted for distribution margins, tax and transport costs, are 40 per cent tariff-equivalent for the EU against 16 per cent for the US. These percentages are not much different if one looks at 1999 instead of his original 1993.

We have updated these figures with the 2002 price data – see the Price Comparison Appendix (Appendix A) – and extended the comparison more widely now that OECD membership has risen to include Korea in particular; we also cover all EU countries and have made an attempt to update the figures relative to China. The figures for the EU weighted average against lowest-cost non-EU trade partners are somewhat lower in 2002; the US, followed by Korea, is most often the lowest price alternative. For the EU as a whole the 2002 figure comes out at 21 per cent, against 30–40 per cent on the narrower basis for the 1990s. For the US, which has also embraced policies of non-tariff protection, the 2002 figure is 6.5 per cent, against middle double-digit percentages in the 1990s.

If one attempts to include China, possible in a crude way for 2002, the implied protection estimates become much larger: 68 per cent for the EU and 48 per cent for the US. These numbers should be treated cautiously because we do not have prices in separate commodity categories for China. The estimates rely on the manufacturing wage cost comparisons made by the US Bureau of Labor Statistics for 2002 (which estimated Chinese manufacturing wage costs per hour at 7 per cent of Korea's); we also assume that unskilled labour represents 30 per cent of total costs, a percentage

Table 4.1   *Survey indicators of service barriers (scale 0–6 from least to most restrictive)*

	1978	1988	1998
UK	4.3	3.5	1.0
RoEU	5.4	5.1	3.4
US	4.0	2.5	1.4
Australia	4.5	4.2	1.6
Canada	4.2	2.8	2.4
Japan	5.2	3.9	2.9
Switzerland	4.5	4.5	3.9

Note: Simple averages of indicators for seven industries – gas, electricity, post, telecoms, air transport, railways and road freight. Depending on the industry the following dimensions have been included: barriers to entry, public ownership, market structure, vertical integration, price controls. For the rest of the EU (RoEU), simple averages of individual EU countries.

Source: Nicoletti and Scarpetta (2001).

Table 4.2   *Estimates of tariff-equivalents on manufactured goods due to all trade barriers (%)*

	1990	1996	1999
Belgium	42	65	42
Germany	39	60	29
Italy	38	36	21
Netherlands	42	58	41
UK	41	41	50
US	16	14	15

Note: Data are expenditure-weighted average ratios of imputed producer prices to the landed prices of goods from the country with the lowest level of price in the sample.

Source: Bradford and Lawrence (2004).

deliberately put on the low, cautious side. Nevertheless, even these crude estimates indicate just how China's products are being kept at bay by various means, at least in finished form. Even as protection may be coming down on the products of the more developed emerging market countries such as Korea, we can see that it is rising in response to the penetration of Chinese products. Nevertheless, China's wage differential is rising as it develops, particularly in the years since the banking crisis when policy has altered to encourage growth in consumption and discourage growth in manufacturing capacity in more outlying regions because of concerns over pollution and excess capacity. So we treat these estimates of protection based on this Chinese data with considerable caution.

Summarizing these measures, we find that by 2002 EU protection may have come down on our preferred measure, based on OECD price comparisons, from a range of 30–40 per cent in the 1990s to 21 per cent by the early 2000s. On the other hand China, not being in the OECD, was not covered in these numbers and against China the protection may have been far greater. Nevertheless, China is itself changing fast, as just noted, and for the sophisticated manufactured products with whose protection the EU is mainly concerned, it has allied itself with Japan and Korea through large supply networks; thus 'made in Japan or Korea' may in practice mean 'assembled from largely Chinese components' in these countries. As with agriculture, we notice a downward trend in protection and again, to avoid an impression of spurious accuracy, we project a continuation of this trend going on to our target year of 2020, where we set the relevant percentage of manufacturing protection also at 10 per cent.

We now turn to our CGE model of trade to obtain measures of the cost to the UK and the EU of this protectionist policy.

First we explain how the model works in outline: details are in the CGE Model Appendix (Appendix B). There is full competition in all products with free entry. There are world markets for the three traded goods, agriculture, manufactures and services; world supply and demand fix the relative prices of these goods, hence two relative prices – of agriculture/manufactures and services/ manufactures. For simplicity we set the world price of manufacturing (relative to which other prices are fixed) at 1. Tariffs (or equivalent measures) raise home prices in the country above their world price. For an individual country therefore prices of traded goods are set in world markets plus the effect of its own tariffs.

We now consider what happens in each country to its supplies and costs. Because of competition, all prices equal marginal costs; hence wages of skilled and unskilled labour and land prices are set by this equality. There are three traded goods and three prices of factors of production that are set in the country. The price of capital is set worldwide and capital circulates at this price to wherever it is needed. For simplicity we set this price as fixed at a constant world real interest rate times a fixed world price of production in manufacturing (of 1); effectively we are assuming that in the long run (the focus of the model), savings are always made available as required at a fixed rate of interest. The wage and land costs, once fixed by traded goods prices, then determine non-traded goods prices.

With all prices set in this way by world prices, tariffs and production technology, we go on to determine how much is produced of each type of good. This is fixed by available supplies of factors of production, namely unskilled and skilled labour. Land, we assume, is provided freely as needed by planners subject to a restriction placed on agricultural land, such that agricultural production is controlled to a fixed amount. Non-traded production has to be equal to non-traded demand, which depends on total GDP and relative non-traded prices. With these restrictions on agriculture and non-traded output we can work out the size of each sector that will exactly exhaust available supplies of the two sorts of labour. Then from that we can work out how much capital and land is needed by each sector.

So to summarize, world prices (determined by world demand and supply by all countries, as resulting from their country solutions) plus tariffs fix country prices and so costs of labour and land. Given these costs and each sector's resulting demands for these factors per unit of output, the sizes of each sector adjust so that the available supplies of the two types of labour are equal to sectoral demands.

So a tariff on manufactures, for example, acts to raise a country's price of manufactures. Then because manufacturing uses a lot of unskilled labour, its expansion drives up unskilled wages. In order to force other industries to economize on the unskilled labour manufacturing needs for its expansion, the other traded sectors contract. The non-traded sector's size moves close to proportionally with the whole economy because demand for non-traded goods is related proportionally to total income, apart from any effect of its changing relative costs brought about by the tariff. The rise in tariff raises consumer prices so that consumers are less well off than they would have been buying the manufactures more cheaply from abroad.

It might seem on the face of it that 10 per cent protection in agriculture and manufacturing is not a very large or significant amount. It raises prices in these two sectors by 10 per cent over the world price, while leaving service prices at world levels. For those used to macro models of short to medium-run behaviour, relative price movements of different sectors of this order occur regularly; for example world raw material prices can double or triple and greatly affect retail prices of sectors using those materials. Yet we do not observe huge sectoral output swings in the economy.

The difference here is that we are computing the long-run effect of permanent relative price changes of these sectors. The sectors with higher prices pay higher wages, both skilled and unskilled, for the workers they need; they pay more for land and they use more capital whose price is fixed in world markets. What our CGE model shows is that resources are heavily attracted out of the service sector into agriculture and manufacturing. In fact we assume that output in agriculture is capped (effectively by control on the land that can be used in this sector) in our model by government policy, so that the attraction into this sector is frustrated by rising land prices. However, for manufacturing, no such limit is placed and the result is a substantial boost to manufacturing at the expense of services.

The effect of raising prices for these two sectors by 10 per cent is first a substantial, 7.5 per cent, rise in the cost of living. Wages of unskilled workers go up more than this, 14 per cent, because they are disproportionately used in manufacturing. But skilled workers' wages fall by 11 per cent, being disproportionately used in service industries. Landowners do well, with land prices soaring by 47 per cent. We see in these figures how the politics of vested interests works; unions representing unskilled workers, farmers and other landowners, as well as manufacturing businesses will clearly support being inside the EU.

Yet the effect of shifting output into sectors where their productivity is less than the price paid by consumers is an overall loss of welfare for UK citizens; these citizens would value more the output lost in services whose production contracts 32 per cent. The loss of welfare, measured by the loss of potential consumption by UK households, is 3.3 per cent. This potential consumption change is measured as the change in the value of all output deflated by its consumer price cost (that is, the change in [nominal GDP/ CPI], minus the change in the value of resources used to generate it).

This cost is computed as if the protective measure is a tariff. However, the customs union acts as a tariff in its effect on outputs and consumption; but the equivalent of the 'tariff revenue' (that is, the extra cost of imports due to the protection) is not paid to the UK government, but rather accrues to foreigners, and we need to make allowances for the effects of this as a transfer of foreign revenues to and from UK citizens. There is revenue on imports from outside the EU; this revenue (paid by UK consumers) accrues to the EU itself as an own resource or else to foreign businesses able to raise their EU prices (via anti-dumping arrangements). At the same time the model assumes that exporters are able to raise their non-EU prices because they can switch their output to satisfying domestic consumers: effectively the model treats non-EU net imports as if these are simply imports, with no exports. These net non-EU imports are small and so we assume there is no loss to UK citizens through this; that is, UK consumers pay more but UK producers get more.

There is also extra revenue accruing to EU businesses that sell protected goods to the UK at higher prices; this revenue is not counted elsewhere and is a cost to UK consumers. Our businesses also gain more from other EU consumers on their exports; so the net revenue paid by UK citizens to other EU citizens is the tariff times the net imports by the UK. On EU trade net imports by the UK are substantial. For manufacturing the UK pays an extra 10 per cent (the assumed tariff-equivalent) on its net imports to its EU partners. For agriculture the workings of the CAP on transfers between countries for agriculture are complex and are already counted in the net UK contribution where they involve money transfers from the EU; but additionally UK consumers pay 10 per cent more (our assumed tariff-equivalent also in agriculture) on their net agricultural imports from the EU just as they do on net manufactured imports. If we put these net transfers together, on net imports of goods from the EU of around 8 per cent of GDP, the net transfer amounts to 10 per cent of this, or 0.8 per cent of GDP. So in sum the total cost to the UK of the protection of agriculture and manufacturing is 4.1 per cent of GDP.

Some politicians attach totemic significance to manufacturing; we heard quite a few arguments after the 2010 election that the economy should be 'rebalanced' towards manufacturing. One can see why protected manufacturing interests would want this; it is no doubt to appeal to these interests that politicians make these arguments. But there is no economic case for encouraging output in sectors which market forces would contract. For such a case there would have to be some disparity between social and market values, yet there is no such disparity. Similar arguments were made two centuries ago for preserving agriculture with a similar lack of basis.

Leaving the EU and eliminating this protection would, according to these figures, raise service output and effectively eliminate manufacturing viewed as the pure making of artefacts. The reason for this is fairly simple: as the UK has developed in the decades since the economy began to be liberalized in 1979, there has been a big rise in the share of skilled labour in the workforce. By now approximately 50 per cent of the cohort of university-age people go on to some form of higher education or equivalent. This has favoured the expansion of skill-intensive industries, of which the service industries are the principal examples. We can also include in these industries the design element of manufacturing, which is a service industry. This element is particularly large in 'hi-tech' manufacturing. These workers are engaged in jobs that require the use of their brainpower and associated skills. The actual making of things, manufacturing in the original sense, has shrunk hugely in the UK, usually to be contracted out to low-wage countries. What the CGE model tells us is that in the absence of EU protection this element would largely disappear. We can note that there is a good demand for unskilled workers in the non-traded service sector (distribution, construction, utilities and so on) which cannot be substituted for by bringing in cheaper substitutes from abroad. As this non-traded sector is around half of the economy, one can see that if roughly half the labour force is unskilled (or semi-skilled, which is included here in

*Table 4.3   Effects of UK tariff of 10% on agriculture and manufacturing:
% changes from base*

% changes	UK	RoEU	NAFTA	ROW
y	−3.99	0.04	0.04	0.03
y_A	0.00	0.00	0.00	0.00
y_M	113.01	−2.17	−2.97	−1.97
y_S	−32.07	1.19	1.13	1.33
y_D	−3.90	0.04	0.04	0.03
E_A	−12.04	0.05	0.09	0.15
E_M	−0.61	0.01	0.01	0.04
E_S	−5.37	0.05	0.05	0.01
w	14.37	−0.19	−0.19	−0.19
h	−11.05	0.66	0.66	0.66
l	47.18	0.11	0.11	0.11
N	1.35	−0.02	−0.02	−0.02
H	−2.48	0.08	0.08	0.08
L	−28.14	0.00	0.01	−0.01
K	6.79	0.07	0.08	0.06
CPI	7.51	0.13	0.13	0.12
P_A	10.07	0.07	0.07	0.07
P_M	10.00	0.00	0.00	0.00
P_S	0.31	0.31	0.31	0.31
Pw_A	0.07	0.07	0.07	0.07
Pw_S	0.31	0.31	0.31	0.31
Welfare	−3.3	−0.00	0.01	−0.01

Notes: Glossary: y=output; E=expenditure; w=wages of unskilled; h=wages of skilled; l=rent on land; N=unskilled labour; H=skilled labour; L=land; K=capital; CPI=consumer prices; P=price of commodity. Suffixes: A=agriculture; M=manufacturing; S=services; W=world.

'unskilled'), it will be fully employed in the non-traded sector and there will be little of it left over for the manufacturing sector. Plainly EU protection, as we have seen, raises the wages of unskilled workers; but if there was a case for redistribution to these workers because they were poor, then this would already be done by public redistribution policy. This policy area is extremely active in the UK, as evidenced by the high progressivity of the tax-benefit system. There is no case for using protection to help carry out this policy since it is clumsily directed at the issue and so, as we have seen, creates a big cost for the economy as a whole.

It turns out that the costs to EU citizens of the EU tariff on agriculture and manufacturing are roughly the same as those for the UK. Thus when the 10 per cent tariff is levied EU-wide, including in the UK, the table of

Table 4.4   Effects of UK+EU tariff of 10% on agriculture and manufacturing: % changes from base

% changes	UK	EU	NAFTA	ROW
y	−3.71	−3.39	0.22	0.16
y_A	0.00	0.00	0.00	0.00
y_M	93.33	49.07	−18.42	−12.22
y_S	−27.02	−30.91	6.97	8.20
y_D	−3.62	−3.47	0.21	0.16
E_A	−11.16	−4.29	0.47	0.76
E_M	−0.56	−0.57	0.03	0.19
E_S	−5.00	−4.76	0.30	0.06
w	13.25	13.25	−1.16	−1.16
h	−8.00	−8.00	4.11	4.11
l	48.37	48.37	0.92	0.92
N	1.25	1.25	−0.12	−0.12
H	−2.06	−2.06	0.52	0.52
L	−28.30	−28.00	−0.18	−0.28
K	7.08	7.75	0.50	0.37
CPI	8.18	8.15	0.79	0.76
P_A	10.48	10.48	0.43	0.43
P_M	10.00	10.00	0.00	0.00
P_S	1.89	1.89	1.89	1.89
Pw_A	0.43	0.43	0.43	0.43
Pw_S	1.89	1.89	1.89	1.89
Welfare	−3.39	−3.00	0.07	−0.03

Note: Glossary as for Table 4.3.

effects shown in Table 4.4 more or less replicate in the rest of the EU what happens in the UK. The only difference for the rest of the EU (RoEU) is that there is a small net revenue gain due to the net revenue transfer from UK to RoEU consumers; but as a percentage of the much larger RoEU GDP total, it is only 0.15 per cent of their GDP. Thus the total welfare cost to RoEU is just under 3 per cent of GDP.

4.2   RESPONDING TO OTHER CALCULATIONS OF EU TRADE COST/BENEFIT

In Chapter 1 we noted the work of Ottaviano et al. (2014), who conclude that leaving the EU would bring, contrary to our estimate of a 4 per cent gain, a loss of some 1 per cent of GDP. This is, to say the least, a surprising finding. It turns out that they treat leaving the EU as merely resulting in a rise of manufacturing tariffs imposed on the UK by the EU, as well as a rise in other barriers to trade with the UK; inside the EU the UK does not face these barriers. However, while this assumption is correct, it ignores the point that after exit the UK would no longer levy tariffs on the rest of the world; it would, as we have explained, leave the EU customs union for free trade. Implicitly, they in effect assume that the UK would maintain the same tariff-equivalent barriers against the ROW if it left the EU; but this would be clearly welfare-reducing compared with going to free trade, as we assume. It is indeed a 'straw man'. In our approach the main gain for the UK in leaving the EU is that it can abandon the mass of complex trade barriers the EU levies on the rest of the world, both in agriculture and in manufacturing.

If Ottaviano et al. had allowed for the total policy discussed here, namely leaving a regional customs union for free trade with the whole world, then their calculations should have come into line with ours. The EU currently levies a substantial tariff-equivalent on the ROW, raising UK prices above world prices. The UK pays more for its imports, including more to its EU partners, and receives no tariff revenue. Its exporters also receive higher prices on EU exports and also, as we have seen, on exports to the ROW because they are interchangeable with imports and EU exports. If the UK leaves the EU these prices fall to world levels. If, as it well might, the EU after UK exit levied on the UK's exports the same tariff-equivalent as on any other ROW suppliers, this would not affect the price the UK gets, which is the world price; it would simply mean that EU consumers would pay this plus the tariff-equivalent (that is, the same price as they paid before). As we have seen, this results in a fall in profitability of EU-protected output relative to output unprotected by the EU. Similar arguments apply to EU exporters to the UK, who would find it no longer so profitable to export to the UK relative to selling at home or to the rest of the EU. In the language of customs union, UK exit ends 'trade diversion' towards EU-protected output and trade. It would certainly be interesting to see the total changes including those on ROW tariffs calculated within a multiple-sector gravity model, since this contains much rich detail of reactions at a highly disaggregated level. Absent the effort to include the ROW, we unfortunately do not have this calculation from Ottaviano et al.

There is a parallel here with the debate a decade ago about the UK joining the euro. Many in favour asserted that joining the euro would eliminate exchange rate uncertainty and so also get rid of a tax on trade and foreign investment. However, they forgot that it would only eliminate regional exchange rate uncertainty. Our work then (it is explained in Chapter 3) showed that because of the euro's substantial fluctuations against the dollar (and hence against most rest of the world currencies), exchange rate uncertainty of the pound against the dollar and the ROW currencies would rise sharply, implying, as we found out from simulations of the relevant variations, that overall exchange rate uncertainty would not necessarily go down and could go up. So here it is true that joining the EU has lowered our trade barriers with the EU but raised them against the ROW. The analogy is not exact because here we are talking about relative price effects (effects on average prices) whereas in the euro case we were discussing uncertainty (the variability of prices). However, the basic point remains, that we must allow for global and not merely regional aspects of the issue.

A further question that arises with the calculations of Ottaviano et al. is that they are not based on a 'structural' general equilibrium model. Even though they claim that the gravity trade model they use, from Costinot and Rodriguez-Clare (2013) (CR), is a good representation of the 'reduced form' (i.e overall) effects of shocks to the world economy like globalization and so can be treated as if it is a general equilibrium model, there is no guarantee it will have the right reduced form effects for a shock to economic trade structure such as leaving a customs union. We know from macro general equilibrium models (and trade models are simply a sub-class) that the reduced form effects of different shocks (the 'impulse response functions') differ, an idea known as Lucas' Critique of reduced form econometric macro models. CR discuss the potential advantages of using multiple-sector gravity models as well as the disadvantages. The latter include the difficulties of pinning down the elasticities that are the workhorse of the gravity model. CR suggest that, in principle, if one is willing to make particular assumptions on utility and production functions and the competitive micro-foundations of the model, a gravity model with the correct elasticities can capture the effect of tariff shocks. However, this raises the question of whether these elasticities can be calculated reliably and are structural in the sense that they do not vary with different policy shocks and regimes. CR admit that there is difficulty in achieving agreement on what the elasticities should be; and it seems plain that they will depend on what constellation of shocks is considered, as well as precisely what relationships the gravity model is based on. After all the elasticity represents the total solved effect of the tariff on trade volume; this will be reached through a complex web of reinforcing and offsetting effects via many channels. A tariff effect when no other tariffs change and when there are no effects on the general level of wages and prices will differ from one when other tariffs change in a complex way and there are large effects on the wage/price structure.

To make the matter concrete, globalization (the main shock CR consider) is like a tide lifting all boats from which one would expect trade to expand and with it GDP in all countries; yet leaving a customs union will cause a reversal of trade diversion so that some UK trade will contract and other trade will expand, while GDP will change structure, with some (small) overall expansion in efficiency. While trade will indeed change direction away from the EU, this will improve the structure of the UK economy and the gains of this need to be evaluated.

Will Leaving the EU Create 'Border' Costs with the EU?

One further element stressed by Ottaviano et al. is the way that invisible barriers to trade, through regulative differences for example, may be raised on UK–EU trade if the UK leaves. This is nowadays called 'the border', as it seems that when borders exist between countries, trade is reduced materially; we discussed this in Chapter 3 in the context of work by McCallum (1995) on the Canadian–US border. However, this assumes a total breakdown of relations between the UK and the EU on UK departure, which is most unlikely. On the contrary, we envisage the signing of a bilateral treaty in which barriers would be kept to the minimum. If UK firms feel that keeping EU regulations in place for their industries would enhance their situation, they are quite free to retain them and not merely on their exports to the EU.

Can one square the circle of leaving the EU and yet maintaining no barriers between the UK and the EU on trade? Plainly from the UK perspective, free trade with all includes the EU and so no barriers to EU imports would be erected by the UK after departure. UK regulative systems would, where UK industry required it, remain the same as the EU system, except in labour markets where we would preserve our own market approach as now, minus some recent EU intrusions. The question is whether the EU would wish to levy barriers against UK imports.

From the EU's viewpoint (misguided as we may find it) the aim is to keep prices within the EU at their protected (target) level, while disrupting as little as possible existing commercial relationships within the industry that cross the UK–EU border. In this aim they will be reinforced by industry lobbying, since this is greatly in the industry's interest also. One possibility is that they could persuade the UK in some cases to abandon free trade and simply preserve the status quo; plainly the UK will come under intense lobbying in some industries to do precisely this. Realism suggests that in a few industries, possibly including the volume car market, lobbyists might succeed in this aim, at least for a transitional period. Notice that this arrangement would be a called a 'free trade agreement' between the UK and the EU in respect of this industry. Really it is the exact opposite of what the name implies, namely a decision to keep existing trade barrier preferences in place.

Another possibility is that the UK would stick to its free trade policy and that the EU would allow continued preferential access by UK-sourced products in the industry – so permitting UK producers to continue to enjoy high prices on EU exports. Presumably there would be an upper limit on the quantity of UK product allowed to enjoy this preference, as otherwise UK capacity would be switched in potentially unlimited quantities into this relatively profitable outlet, given that general costs have fallen.

Yet a further possibility is that the pressure of UK competition would eventually lead to the EU's abandoning of its preferential barriers.

Or finally the EU might decide on none of the above and simply treat the UK like the ROW, raising trade barriers against it. In effect our calculations assume this last decision, so that UK industries all face world prices in all their markets. Notice, however, that there is no assumption here of any regulative barrier; the barriers would simply mean that the UK would pay a trade tax that would raise its EU prices above world prices by the same margin as currently occurring within the EU. Subject to paying this tax there would be no 'invisible border' barrier between the UK and the EU.

It is difficult to predict which of these outcomes will be chosen in every industrial case. However, we should make it quite clear that from the viewpoint of general economic welfare the best outcome is full free trade, with the EU treating us like the ROW and raising its existing preferential tariff-equivalent. This outcome would ensure that the UK moved to world prices, under which it would enjoy its comparative advantage and therefore its economy would be the least distorted. It is this calculation that we have made in assessing the cost of EU trade membership. As noted, we see no reason to deduct from this any cost of some 'invisible' barrier since we can see no such barrier being involved.

Should other outcomes be chosen, in effect these would lead to less political obstruction of the UK's decision to leave the EU but also less gain from doing so. We think such outcomes may well be transitional elements in any agreement, as discussed elsewhere in this book. So our assumption is that they may well occur in some case temporarily but do not affect the long-term gains.

4.3 CONCLUSIONS

What we have seen in this chapter is that the EU protects agriculture and manufacturing through its commercial policies, namely its tariffs, its non-tariff barriers and the Common Agricultural Policy. In this book we have devoted many pages to describing these policies, in later chapters and in this summary chapter whose aim is to pull all these figures together into a form that can give us an overall cost to the economy. In sum these policies are designed to satisfy numerous vested interests in the countries of the EU; these interests include organized unskilled labour, the industries where this labour is most used, farmers and landowners. Service industries, skilled workers and consumers have little voice in the councils of the EU, as is usually found in studies of the political economy of lobbying. The reason is that they are dispersed, poorly organized, or have only recently grown in size. The policies that pander to the voices of powerful vested interests, however, damage the economy as a whole. This is as true of the rest of the EU as it is of the UK. So one might ask why we should not engage with the rest of the EU to rectify the matter. But of course the problem is that the EU is not organized in a way that can defeat such interests. Instead it seems to be well structured for these interests to prevail through the power of lobbying, which is stronger than the political power behind greater competition and free trade. In the UK, by contrast, the Parliamentary system has enabled reforms to take place that have favoured competition; a public debate has flourished over the past three and a half decades that has empowered consumers, skilled workers and the wide swathe of service industries, including most importantly the City of London. Because liberalization has brought growth and full employment, a consensus has formed behind policies of further liberalization and general 'wealth creation' through free markets and free trade. An important element of this consensus is the acceptance that those who lose out in a significant way should be compensated through the tax-benefit system or in severe cases by special subventions to groups or regions. By leaving the EU, the UK would be able to abandon the EU's protectionist system in favour of free trade combined with transitional compensation for those hit by the changes. This would raise economic welfare by around 4 per cent and enhance the shift of the UK economy away from manufacturing into service (and hi-tech) industries where UK growth has been concentrated largely in the decades since 1979.

APPENDIX A: PRICE COMPARISON TO CALCULATE PROTECTION

Bradford (2003) presented new measures of final goods trade protection in eight developed countries. He argued that the barriers to arbitrage between countries are barriers to trade. To measure the trade barriers, one needs to allow for unavoidable costs associated with shipping goods between countries. Once this is done, if there is a price gap for equivalent goods in two different countries, then the higher-price market is protected. To measure the protection barriers, one needs to use the factory prices of the good, not the retail prices. These factory/producer prices show which industries in which countries are most efficient.

Data

The data are collected by the OECD in order to calculate purchasing-power parity (PPP) estimates. We use the basic-heading price data published for the year 2002. All prices were converted to US dollars. The margins are calculated using the data from the latest national input–output tables, published for the year 2000. Given the list of prices of the goods and services in the OECD PPP data, we have to find the equivalent margins from the national input–output tables, but the two lists are not identical, so we have to find the best match by aggregating different products and services. For example, in the PPP list there are separate categories for engines and turbines, pumps and compressors, other general-purpose machinery and so on; we aggregate them all to get the equivalent of manufacture of machinery except electrical in the input–output tables.

Calculating Protection Levels

The price data obtained for the OECD countries are consumer prices, not the producer prices that one needs to measure how much an industry is insulated from the world market. These consumer prices are converted to producer prices using data on distribution margins, which include wholesale trade, retail trade and transportation costs. The method involves three steps.

First, given the consumer prices, one produces estimates of producer prices by peeling off the ad valorem margin, which is defined as the ratio of the value of output in consumer prices to the value of output in producer prices:

$$p_{ij}^p = \frac{p_{ij}^c}{1 + m_{ij}}$$

where

p_{ij}^p = producer price of good i in country j,
p_{ij}^c = consumer price of good i in country j, as taken from the OECD data,
m_{ij} = margin for good i in country j, as taken from the national input–output table.

Second, account must be taken of transport costs from one nation's market to another, as these insulate the market from foreign competition. The world price is derived using data on the export margin and international transport costs. The idea is that to be sold in the domestic market, a foreign good must travel from the foreign factory to the foreign border and then to the domestic border. The domestic producer price must be compared with the landed price of the foreign good (world price). Adding the export margins to the producer prices generates the export price for each good in each country:

$$p_{ij}^e = p_{ij}^p(1 + em_{ij}),$$

where

p_{ij}^e = export price of good i for country j,
em_{ij} = export margin of good i for country j.
The world price is found by adding the international transport cost to the lowest export price in the sample:

$$p_i^w = p_{iM}(1 + tm_i),$$

where

p_i^w = world price of good i,
$p_{iM} = \min(p_{i1}^e, \ldots, p_{in}^e)$, the minimum of all export prices,
tm_i = the international transport margin for good i.

Finally, the ratio of each country's producer price to the world price indicates a preliminary measure of protection, ppr_{ij}

$$ppr_{ij} = \frac{p_{ij}^p}{p_i^w}.$$

Example: Figure 4A.1 illustrates the above calculation procedure for the manufacture of cars and other road equipment in two countries.

To find the world price in the manufacture of cars and other road equipment across the countries, first for each country we turn the consumer price into a producer price by dividing the consumer price by the

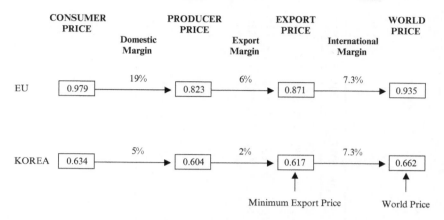

*Figure 4A.1   The calculation procedure: example for cars and other road
equipment*

domestic margin plus 1. Second, recognizing that goods must travel and
be transported from one country to another, we use the export margin
to calculate the export price of the goods (multiplying the producer price
by the export margin plus 1) and see which country has the lowest export
price in the category. This price is then used in combination with the
international transport margin to derive the world price of this manufacturing category. The protection measure of each country is then just the
ratio of that country's producer price to the world price. In the example,
the protection measure for the manufacture of cars and other road equipment in the EU area is $\frac{0.823}{0.662}$ = 1.243, thus protection of 24.3 per cent.

We apply the above calculation across manufacturing sectors to compare
the competitiveness between the EU area, Korea and the USA. We report
all the steps (see Tables 4A.1 to 4A.8).

Table 4A.1   PPPs

	AUT	BEL	FIN	FRA	GER	IRL	ITA	NLD	PRT	SPA	DK	SWE	UK	KOR	US	EU
Textiles	1.22	0.96	0.62	0.71	0.79	0.87	0.67	1.09	0.4	0.62	0.78	0.68	1.07	0.57	1	0.81
Printing, publishing and allied industries	1.03	1.03	0.83	1.54	0.66	0.97	1	1.08	0.95	0.93	0.86	0.82	0.78	0.95	1	0.97
Machinery except electrical	1.27	1.3	1.31	1.48	1.32	1.39	1.22	1.25	1.23	1.2	1.45	1.35	1.41	1.04	1	1.33
Electrical machinery apparatus, appliances and supplies	1.2	1.21	1.33	1.31	1.34	1.39	1.04	1.33	1.38	1.14	1.34	1.02	1.3	1.25	1	1.25
Medical, precision and optical instruments, watches and clocks	1.08	0.93	1.16	1.24	1.15	1.19	1.26	0.94	2.47	1.08	0.99	1.12	1.18	1.04	1	1.17
Transport equipment*	1	0.92	1.18	0.99	0.96	1.12	0.87	0.98	1.04	0.89	1.39	0.95	1.02	0.65	1	0.97
Furniture and other	1.39	1.33	1.33	1.55	1.6	1.36	1.55	1.33	1.46	1.18	1.05	1.21	1.47	0.6	1	1.47

Notes:
* Excluding aircraft, helicopters, hovercraft and other aeronautical equipment due to unclear data.
Food, Beverages and Tobacco is excluded from the calculation because we do not have the necessary data for New Zealand, which is known as the most efficient producer of processed food.

Table 4A.2   Domestic margins

	AUT	BEL	FIN	FRA	GER	IRL	ITA	NLD	PRT	SPA	DK	SWE	UK	KOR	US	EU
Textiles	1.54	1.19	1.59	1.26	1.45	1.24	1.23	1.28	1.19	1.28	1.41	1.55	1.48	1.31	1.38	1.36
Printing, publishing and allied industries	1.27	1.10	1.33	1.37	1.16	1.05	1.42	0.96	1.22	1.23	1.20	1.17	1.26	1.19	1.12	1.24
Machinery except electrical	1.21	1.21	1.11	1.18	1.14	1.05	1.16	1.24	1.25	1.18	1.30	1.02	1.17	1.07	1.28	1.17
Electrical machinery apparatus, appliances and supplies	1.13	1.17	1.09	1.15	1.13	1.04	1.17	0.88	1.16	1.15	1.22	1.09	1.27	1.07	1.29	1.15
Medical, precision and optical instruments, watches and clocks	1.44	1.22	1.22	1.22	1.27	1.03	1.27	1.52	1.34	1.24	1.29	1.19	1.21	1.17	1.19	1.26
Transport equipment*	1.18	1.15	1.45	1.15	1.10	1.37	1.25	1.33	1.27	1.13	1.60	1.15	1.21	1.05	1.20	1.19
Furniture and other	1.47	1.21	1.67	1.56	1.58	1.85	1.51	1.16	1.50	1.41	1.35	1.51	1.79	1.21	1.84	1.54

Notes:
* Excluding aircraft, helicopters, hovercraft and other aeronautical equipment due to unclear data.
Domestic Margin is identified as the ratio of the total use at purchasers' prices in the use table and the total use at basic prices in the input–output table.

Source: National Input–Output tables.

Table 4A.3 *Producer prices*

	AUT	BEL	FIN	FRA	GER	IRL	ITA	NLD	PRT	SPA	DK	SWE	UK	KOR	US	EU**
Textiles	0.80	0.81	0.39	0.56	0.55	0.70	0.54	0.85	0.33	0.48	0.56	0.44	0.72	0.44	0.72	0.60
Printing, publishing and allied industries	0.81	0.93	0.62	1.13	0.57	0.93	0.70	1.13	0.78	0.75	0.72	0.70	0.62	0.79	0.89	0.78
Machinery except electrical	1.05	1.08	1.18	1.25	1.16	1.33	1.04	1.01	0.98	1.02	1.11	1.32	1.21	0.98	0.78	1.14
Electrical machinery apparatus, appliances and supplies	1.06	1.04	1.23	1.14	1.18	1.33	0.88	1.51	1.19	0.98	1.11	0.93	1.02	1.17	0.78	1.09
Medical, precision and optical instruments, watches and clocks	0.75	0.76	0.95	1.01	0.90	1.16	1.00	0.62	1.84	0.87	0.77	0.94	0.98	0.89	0.84	0.93
Transport equipment*	0.85	0.80	0.81	0.86	0.88	0.82	0.70	0.74	0.81	0.79	0.86	0.82	0.84	0.61	0.83	0.82
Furniture and other	0.95	1.10	0.80	1.00	1.01	0.73	1.03	1.15	0.97	0.83	0.78	0.80	0.82	0.50	0.54	0.95

Notes:
* Excluding aircraft, helicopters, hovercraft and other aeronautical equipment due to unclear data.
** Weighted by GDP.
Producer price = PPP/Domestic Margin.

Table 4A.4 Export margins

	AUT	BEL	FIN	FRA	GER	IRL	ITA	NLD	PRT	SPA	DK	SWE	UK	KOR	US	EU**
Textiles	1.09	1.07	1.05	1.03	1.06	1.00	1.10	0.98	1.00	1.15	1.12	1.03	1.15	1.06	1.07	1.07
Printing, publishing and allied industries	1.04	1.06	0.82	1.06	1.02	1.00	1.10	0.83	1.00	1.17	1.03	1.01	1.12	1.06	1.05	1.05
Machinery except electrical	1.09	1.12	0.97	1.07	1.06	1.00	1.04	1.12	1.00	1.09	1.10	1.11	1.08	1.05	1.07	1.07
Electrical machinery apparatus, appliances and supplies	1.02	1.08	0.83	1.06	1.05	1.00	1.04	0.92	1.00	1.07	1.12	1.03	1.14	1.03	1.05	1.05
Medical, precision and optical instruments, watches and clocks	1.11	1.10	1.01	1.08	1.08	1.00	1.04	1.55	1.00	1.06	1.21	1.08	1.11	1.11	1.10	1.10
Transport equipment*	1.01	1.06	1.02	1.02	1.02	1.00	1.08	1.38	1.00	1.04	1.14	1.06	1.04	1.02	1.06	1.06
Furniture and other	1.06	1.08	1.04	1.12	1.06	1.01	1.10	1.05	1.00	1.07	1.07	1.09	1.10	1.10	1.08	1.08

Notes:
* Excluding aircraft, helicopters, hovercraft and other aeronautical equipment due to unclear data.
** Weighted by GDP.
The export margins are available from national input–output tables – the difference between exports at purchasers' prices in the use table and exports at basic prices by product in the input–output table.

Source: National Input–Output and Use tables.

Table 4A.5 Export prices

	AUT	BEL	FIN	FRA	GER	IRL	ITA	NLD	PRT	SPA	DK	SWE	UK	KOR	US	EU**
Textiles	0.87	0.87	0.41	0.58	0.58	0.7	0.6	0.83	0.33	0.55	0.62	0.45	0.83	0.46	0.78	0.64
Printing, publishing and allied industries	0.84	0.99	0.51	1.2	0.59	0.93	0.77	0.94	0.78	0.88	0.75	0.71	0.69	0.84	0.94	0.82
Machinery except electrical	1.14	1.21	1.15	1.35	1.23	1.33	1.09	1.13	0.98	1.12	1.22	1.47	1.31	1.03	0.84	1.22
Electrical machinery apparatus, appliances and supplies	1.09	1.12	1.02	1.21	1.24	1.33	0.92	1.39	1.19	1.06	1.24	0.96	1.16	1.21	0.82	1.15
Medical, precision and optical instruments, watches and clocks	0.83	0.84	0.96	1.09	0.97	1.16	1.03	0.96	1.84	0.92	0.93	1.01	1.09	0.99	0.92	1.03
Transport equipment*	0.86	0.84	0.83	0.88	0.89	0.82	0.75	1.02	0.81	0.82	0.98	0.88	0.88	0.63	0.88	0.86
Furniture and other	1.01	1.19	0.82	1.11	1.07	0.74	1.14	1.2	0.97	0.89	0.83	0.87	0.91	0.55	0.59	1.03

Notes:
* Excluding aircraft, helicopters, hovercraft and other aeronautical equipment due to unclear data.
** Weighted by GDP.
Export Price = Producer Price * Export Margin.

Table 4.4.6   *Transport margins*

	AUT	BEL	FIN	FRA	GER	IRL	ITA	NLD	PRT	SPA	DK	SWE	UK	KOR	US	EU**
Textiles	1.15	1.15	1.15	1.15	1.15	1.15	1.15	1.15	1.15	1.15	1.15	1.15	1.15	1.15	1.15	1.15
Printing, publishing and allied industries	1.20	1.20	1.20	1.20	1.20	1.20	1.20	1.20	1.20	1.20	1.20	1.20	1.20	1.20	1.20	1.20
Machinery except electrical	1.07	1.07	1.07	1.07	1.07	1.07	1.07	1.07	1.07	1.07	1.07	1.07	1.07	1.07	1.07	1.07
Electrical machinery apparatus, appliances and supplies	1.07	1.07	1.07	1.07	1.07	1.07	1.07	1.07	1.07	1.07	1.07	1.07	1.07	1.07	1.07	1.07
Medical, precision and optical instruments, watches and clocks	1.07	1.07	1.07	1.07	1.07	1.07	1.07	1.07	1.07	1.07	1.07	1.07	1.07	1.07	1.07	1.07
Transport equipment*	1.07	1.07	1.07	1.07	1.07	1.07	1.07	1.07	1.07	1.07	1.07	1.07	1.07	1.07	1.07	1.07
Furniture and other	1.13	1.13	1.13	1.13	1.13	1.13	1.13	1.13	1.13	1.13	1.13	1.13	1.13	1.13	1.13	1.13

Notes:
*   Excluding aircraft, helicopters, hovercraft and other aeronautical equipment due to unclear data.
** Weighted by GDP.

Transport Margin = US cif value of imports/US fob value of imports; the cif values are in the input–output table clearly, but the fob values are in the customs value/international merchandise data; the US transport margin is used as the international transport margin for all countries, where the transport margins in the four equipment manufacturing sectors is the average of international transport margins of machinery except electrical, electrical machinery and transport equipment sectors.

Table 4A.7 World prices

	AUT	BEL	FIN	FRA	GER	IRL	ITA	NLD	PRT	SPA	DK	SWE	UK	KOR	US	EU**
Textiles	1.00	1.00	0.47	0.67	0.67	0.81	0.69	0.96	0.39	0.64	0.72	0.52	0.95	0.53	0.90	0.74
Printing, publishing and allied industries	1.01	1.18	0.61	1.44	0.70	1.12	0.92	1.12	0.94	1.06	0.89	0.85	0.83	1.01	1.12	0.98
Machinery except electrical	1.22	1.30	1.23	1.45	1.32	1.43	1.17	1.21	1.05	1.20	1.31	1.58	1.41	1.10	0.90	1.31
Electrical machinery apparatus, appliances and supplies	1.17	1.21	1.09	1.30	1.33	1.43	0.99	1.49	1.28	1.14	1.33	1.04	1.25	1.30	0.88	1.23
Medical, precision and optical instruments, watches and clocks	0.89	0.90	1.03	1.17	1.04	1.24	1.11	1.03	1.98	0.99	1.00	1.08	1.17	1.06	0.99	1.10
Transport equipment*	0.92	0.90	0.89	0.94	0.96	0.88	0.81	1.09	0.87	0.88	1.05	0.94	0.95	0.89	0.94	0.93
Furniture and other	1.14	1.35	0.93	1.26	1.21	0.84	1.29	1.36	1.10	1.01	0.94	0.99	1.02	0.62	0.66	1.17

Notes:
*   Excluding aircraft, helicopters, hovercraft and other aeronautical equipment due to unclear data.
** Weighted by GDP.
Producer Price after taking off all the Margins = Export Price * International Transport Margin = World Price.

Table 4A.8   Weighted average protection rates for the EU and the US

	US	EU**
Textiles	1.36	1.12
Printing, publishing and allied industries	1.00	1.00
Machinery except electrical	1.00	1.27
Electrical machinery apparatus, appliances and supplies	1.00	1.24
Medical, precision and optical instruments, watches and clocks	1.00	1.00
Transport equipment*	1.23	1.22
Furniture and other	1.00	1.54
Weighted	1.07	1.21

Notes:
* Excluding aircraft, helicopters, hovercraft and other aeronautical equipment due to unclear data.
** Weighted by GDP.
Protection = Domestic Producer Price / World Price.

APPENDIX B: THE COMPUTABLE GENERAL EQUILIBRIUM MODEL FOR TRADE

The model we have used for the evaluation of general equilibrium effects of trade policy is based on one we developed for assessing the effects of globalization on the world economy (Minford et al., 1997). This model performed well empirically in accounting for the trade trends of the 1970–90 period. We identified a group of major causal 'shocks' during this period, which between them gave a good fit to the salient features of the period – including terms of trade, production shares, sectoral trade balances, relative wage movements and employment/unemployment trends.

The model adopts the key assumptions of the Heckscher–Ohlin–Samuelson set-up. Production functions are assumed to be Cobb–Douglas and identical across countries, up to a differing productivity multiplier factor; thus factor shares are constant, enabling us to calibrate the model parsimoniously from detailed UK data that we were able to gather. There are four sectors: non-traded, and three traded ones: primary, basic (unskilled-labour-intensive) manufacturing, and services and other (skilled-labour-intensive) manufacturing. Three immobile factors of production are identified: unskilled and skilled labour and land. Capital is mobile. All sectors are competitive and prices of traded goods of each sector are equalized across borders.

This set-up gives rise to a well-known set of equations (see below for a full listing):

1. Given world prices of traded goods, price = average costs determine the prices of immobile factors of productions.
2. These factor prices induce domestic supplies of these factors.
3. Outputs of each sector are determined by these immobile factor supplies; non-traded sector output is fixed by demand, the traded sector outputs by the supplies of immobile factors not used in the non-traded sector.
4. Demands for traded goods are set by the resulting level of total GDP.
5. World prices are set by world demand = world supply.

The world is divided into four blocs: UK, RoEU (rest of EU), US + rest of NAFTA, ROW (rest of world). Data for the model base run are taken from 1998, the latest generally-available information that was comprehensive at the time we started this work.

In each country we assume that for the primary sector output is politic-ally controlled (for example by quotas) because of the high degree of protection of agriculture and the accompanying requirement to limit the extent of output response. The supply of land is adjusted (via planning and other controls) to adjust to this and other output requirements; in other words the supply of land is demand-determined. While this assumption is crude in overriding all incentive effects on output, the reality of agricultural production is closer to this than to the uncontrolled alternative; we were unable to implement any finer assumption.

Listing of the General Equilibrium 4-bloc Trade Model

1–4 Prices, UK, Rest of EU, NAFTA, Rest of World p_M, p_S, p_A, p_D. p_M, p_S, p_A, p_D domestic prices, solve for w, h, l and p_D respectively.

$$p_M = w^{0.52234} \cdot h^{0.14366} \cdot l^{0.035} \cdot (p_M \cdot r)^{0.299} \cdot \pi_M^{-1}$$

$$p_S = w^{0.21168} \cdot h^{0.51832} \cdot l^{0.033} \cdot (p_M \cdot r)^{0.237} \cdot \pi_S^{-1}$$

$$p_A = w^{0.147} \cdot h^{0.132} \cdot l^{0.079} \cdot (p_M \cdot r)^{0.642} \cdot \pi_A^{-1}$$

$$p_D = w^{0.38024} \cdot h^{0.17576} \cdot l^{0.113} \cdot (p_M \cdot r)^{0.331} \cdot \pi_D^{-1}$$

$$\ln(w) = \left(\frac{1}{0.52234}\right) \cdot \{\ln|(p_M \cdot \pi_M) - 0.14366 \cdot \ln(h)$$
$$- 0.035 \cdot \ln(l) - 0.299 \cdot \ln(p_M \cdot r)\}$$

$$\ln(h) = \left(\frac{1}{0.518324}\right) \cdot \{\ln(p_S \cdot \pi_S) - 0.21168 \cdot \ln(w) - 0.033 \cdot \ln(l)$$
$$- 0.237 \cdot \ln(p_M \cdot r)\}$$

$$\ln(l) = \left(\frac{1}{0.079}\right) \cdot \{\ln(p_A \cdot \pi_A) - 0.147 \cdot \ln(w) - 0.132 \cdot \ln(h)$$
$$- 0.642 \cdot \ln(p_M \cdot r)\}$$

5–7 Factor demands, UK, Rest of EU, NAFTA, Rest of World N, H, L:

$$N = w^{-1} \cdot (0.38024 \cdot p_D \cdot y_D + 0.52234 \cdot y_M \cdot p_M + 0.21168 \cdot p_S \cdot y_S$$
$$+ 0.147 \cdot p_A \cdot y_A)$$

$$H = h^{-1} \cdot (0.168 \cdot p_D \cdot y_D + 0.14366 \cdot y_M \cdot p_M + 0.51832 \cdot p_S \cdot y_S$$
$$+ 0.132 \cdot p_A \cdot y_A)$$

$$L = l^{-1} \cdot (0.113 \cdot p_D \cdot y_D + 0.035 \cdot y_M \cdot p_M + 0.033 \cdot p_S \cdot y_S$$

$$+ \; 0.079 \cdot p_A \cdot y_A)$$

$$y_M = \left(\frac{1}{0.52234 \cdot p_M} \right) \cdot \{ N \cdot w - 0.38024 \cdot p_D \cdot y_D - 0.21168 \cdot p_S \cdot y_S$$

$$- \; 0.147 \cdot p_A \cdot y_A \}$$

$$y_S = \left(\frac{1}{0.51832 \cdot p_S} \right) \cdot \{ H \cdot h - 0.168 \cdot p_D \cdot y_D - 0.14366 \cdot p_M \cdot y_M$$

$$- \; 0.132 \cdot p_A \cdot y_A \}$$

$$y_A^{UK} = 24.62$$

$$y_A^{EU14} = 257.89$$

$$y_A^{NAFTA} = 246.33$$

$$y_A^{RofW} = 1658.32$$

8 *K*

$$K = 0.2 \cdot \frac{1}{(p_M \cdot r)} \cdot \{ 0.331 \cdot p_D \cdot y_D + 0.299 \cdot p_M \cdot y_M$$

$$+ \; 0.237 \cdot p_S \cdot y_S + 0.642 \cdot p_A \cdot y_A \} + 0.8 \cdot K_{t-1}$$

9–11 Factor supplies:

$$N = a_N \cdot \left(\frac{w}{b} \right)^{0.1} \cdot POP^{0.5} \cdot G^{0.5}$$

$$a_N^{UK} = 803.48$$

$$a_N^{EU14} = 4490.02$$

$$a_N^{NAFTA} = 6494.97$$

$$a_N^{RofW} = 13270.9$$

$$H = a_H \cdot \left(\frac{h}{w} \right)^{0.1} \cdot G^{0.5}$$

$$a_H^{UK} = 743.05$$

$$a_H^{EU14} = 3602.76$$

$$a_H^{NAFTA} = 5531.12$$

$$a_H^{RofW} = 9925.96$$

$$L = l^{-1} \cdot (0.113 \cdot p_D \cdot y_D + 0.035 \cdot y_M \cdot p_M + 0.033 \cdot p_S \cdot y_S + 0.079 \cdot p_A \cdot y_A)$$

12 y_D

$$y_D = 0.50 \cdot E^{1.0} \cdot \left(\frac{p_D}{p_T}\right)^{-0.5}$$

13 y

$$y = y_D + y_M + y_S + y_A$$

14 E

$$E = y$$

15 C

$$C = E - \Delta K$$

16 E_T

$$E_T = E - y_D - BOP$$

17 E_M

$$E_M = E_T - E_S - E_A$$

18 E_S

$$E_S^{UK} = 0.9 \cdot E_T^{UK} - 319.12 - 12.0 \cdot (p_S^{UK} - p_T^{UK})$$

$$E_S^{EU14} = 0.9 \cdot E_T^{EU14} - 1551.58 - 12.0 \cdot (p_S^{EU14} - p_T^{EU14})$$

$$E_S^{NAFTA} = 0.9 \cdot E_T^{NAFTA} - 2595.25 - 12.0 \cdot (p_S^{NAFTA} - p_T^{NAFTA})$$

$$E_S^{RofW} = 0.212 \cdot E_T^{RofW} + 7138.97 - 3.0 \cdot (p_S^{RofW} - p_T^{RofW})$$

19 E_A

$$E_A^{UK} = 0.05 \cdot E_T^{UK} - 39.82 - 5.0 \cdot (p_A^{UK} - p_T^{UK})$$

$$E_A^{EU14} = 0.05 \cdot E_T^{EU14} - 53.63 - 5.0 \cdot (p_A^{EU14} - p_T^{EU14})$$

$$E_A^{NAFTA} = 0.05 \cdot E_T^{NAFTA} - 264.24 - 5.0 \cdot (p_A^{NAFYA} - p_T^{NAFTA})$$

$$E_A^{RofW} = 0.413 \cdot E_T^{RofW} - 6075.95 - 15.0 \cdot (p_A^{RofW} - p_T^{RofW})$$

20 p

$$p = p_M \cdot \left(\frac{E_M^{base}}{E^{base}}\right) + p_S \cdot \left(\frac{E_S^{base}}{E^{base}}\right) + p_A \cdot \left(\frac{E_A^{base}}{E^{base}}\right) + p_D \cdot \left(\frac{E_T^{base}}{E^{base}}\right)$$

21–23 p_M, p_S, p_A

$$p_M = p_M^{World} \cdot (1 + T_M)$$

$$p_S = p_S^{World} \cdot (1 + T_S)$$

$$p_A = p_A^{World} \cdot (1 + T_A)$$

World prices. Sums are over four blocs.
Variables without superscripts are bloc variables.
p_A^{World} is derived from the relationship:

$$\sum y_A = \sum E_A$$

The RHS is expanded using the expression for E_A in Equation (19) and the expression for p_A in Equation (27). a_1, a_2 and a_3 are the coefficients from the RHS of the equation for E_A:

$$\sum y_A = \sum \{a_1 \cdot E_T + a_2 + a_3 \cdot (p_A - p_T)\}$$

$$\sum y_A = \sum \{a_1 \cdot E_T + a_2 + a_3 \cdot (1 + T_A) \cdot p_A^{World} = a_3 \cdot p_T\}$$

$$\sum y_A = \sum \{a_1 \cdot E_T + a_2 - a_3 \cdot p_T\} + p_A^{World} \cdot \sum a_3 \cdot (1 + T_A)$$

$$p_A^{World} = \frac{\sum y_A - \sum \{a_1 \cdot E_T - a_2 + a_3 \cdot p_T\}}{\sum a_3 \cdot (1 + T_A)}$$

p_A^{World} is derived similarly.

b_1, b_2 and b_3 are the coefficients from the RHS of the equation for E_S:

$$\sum y_S = \sum E_S$$

and

$$p_S^{World} = \frac{\sum y_S - \sum \{b_1 \cdot E_T - b_2 + b_3 \cdot p_T\}}{\sum b_3 \cdot (1 + T_S)}$$

Glossary: y=output; E=expenditure; w=wages of unskilled; h=wages of skilled; l=rent on land; N=unskilled labour; H=skilled labour; L=land; K=capital; CPI=consumer prices; P=price of commodity. Suffixes: A=agriculture; M=manufacturing; S=services; W=world; BOP= current account balance.

PART II

Recent trade developments: facts and analysis

5. Agriculture

Given the wave of liberalization and reform in the last three decades, restrictions on agricultural trade have declined from the high levels of the 1980s, even though barriers to agricultural trade remain significant in developed countries. Agriculture is protected by tariff barriers, production support and the use of export subsidies in many countries. Very few of these price distortions can be explained as being required to deal with market failures.

Developed economies account for nearly 80 per cent of agricultural market distortions, as measured by world price effects. However, even among developed countries, support levels vary widely. In general – and unsurprisingly – support is smallest in countries that have efficient, export-oriented sectors (notably, Australia and New Zealand) and largest in those that are relatively inefficient and compete with imports (Japan, Korea, the EU). The EU accounts for 38 per cent of world price distortions, compared to Japan plus Korea (12 per cent), the US (16 per cent), and Canada (2 per cent). Among the numerous distortions in international agricultural trade, those imposed by the EU are the most disruptive, resulting in substantial welfare costs for the EU itself and for the world economy generally.

Under the Common Agricultural Policy (CAP) the EU has switched from being a large net importer of agricultural products to a large exporter in the last two decades. The EU's agricultural exports are driven by input cost reductions from subsidies to EU farmers and this has imposed substantial costs on the EU itself and on agricultural exporters in the rest of the world. It has resulted in production surpluses, together with artificially depressed and volatile world prices. These low prices have also created tensions between the major industrial countries, which have found their budgets for agricultural subsidies escalating.

This chapter analyses the issues surrounding the impact of the EU's trade barriers in agriculture and explores the welfare costs of agricultural protection. The first section considers the role of agriculture in developed economies. The second section reviews the data on trade volumes and prices of agricultural goods. The third section describes the level and evolution of barriers to trade in agriculture in the EU and the US in recent years. The fourth section presents estimates of trade barriers which take into account both tariff and non-tariff barriers. The final section outlines the main empirical findings concerning the welfare effects of trade liberalization. An analysis is made of the benefits to EU, NAFTA and the rest of the world if protectionist policies are removed.

5.1   THE ROLE OF AGRICULTURE IN THE ECONOMY

Agriculture's contribution to GDP in the countries of the EU is low – below 3 per cent, with the exception of Bulgaria, Lithuania and Romania – and it is decreasing (Figure 5.1). Between 2000 and 2012 it fell from an average of 2.6 per cent to 1.3 per cent in the core countries of the EU (France, Germany, Italy, United Kingdom and Ireland). In other developed countries, agriculture accounts for 1 per cent in Switzerland and less than 2 per cent in the United States and Japan.

As for employment, agriculture (and hunting, forestry and fishery activity) accounted for around 5.2 per cent of civilian employment in the EU-27 member states in 2012, with the highest in Greece and Poland at 12 per cent. There are close to 1 million farmers in Italy and 0.7 million each

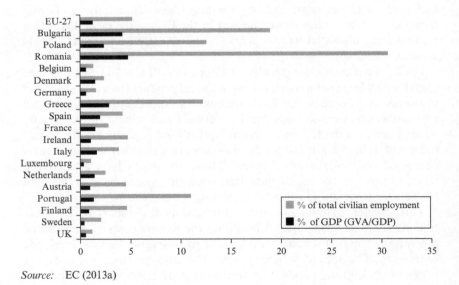

Source: EC (2013a)

Figure 5.1   EU agriculture: basic statistics for 2012

in France and Spain, but they account for only 3 per cent to 4 per cent of total employment. Despite the entry into the EU in 2007 of countries like Bulgaria and Romania, where farmers account for respectively 19 per cent and 30 per cent of the workforce – more farmers than Germany, France, Italy and Spain combined – the share of agriculture in total employment in the EU declined from 5.8 per cent in 2006 to 5.2 per cent in 2012. This is due to the significant fall in the agricultural employment share in other countries such as Italy (from 4.3 per cent in 2006 to 3.8 per cent in 2012), Poland (15.8 per cent in 2006 to 12.6 per cent in 2012) and France (from 3.9 per cent in 2006 to 2.8 per cent in 2012). While agriculture's share of GDP and employment is small, it uses a major share of land and water resources, accounting for nearly 40 per cent of land use and over 40 per cent of water usage in the OECD area.

As for the UK, the total value of its agricultural output is estimated at EUR 10.3 billion in 2012 (£8.1 billion), representing 0.7 per cent of GDP. Milk production is nearly 16.4 per cent of total agricultural produce in the UK, followed by cattle (16.3 per cent), cereals (14 per cent) and poultry (9 per cent). The sector employs 354 000 people (1.2 per cent of the total workforce) and accounts for about 70 per cent of the total land area of the UK. Nearly half of the holdings are small and probably part-time.

5.2 TRADE VOLUMES, PRICES AND HOUSEHOLD CONSUMPTION

The share of agricultural trade in total world trade has declined from 30 per cent in the 1950s to less than 10 per cent in the 1990s and to 8 per cent in 2012. However, agriculture's importance remains greater in trade terms than in output terms (that is, in share of GDP). Imports and exports of agricultural goods account for approximately 6 per cent respectively of merchandise imports and 7 per cent of merchandise exports in the EU (Table 5.1). In the last two decades, the EU export shares of individual commodities in world trade have come down but were still substantial in 2011: wine (21.3 per cent), milk powder (18.1 per cent), cheese (13.4 per cent), butter (8.2 per cent), wheat (12.3 per cent), and sugar (4.2 per cent).

Most of the trade in agricultural products occurs among developed countries, a major part being intra-EU trade (around a quarter of world agricultural trade). In 2012, intra-EU agricultural exports had a value of US$ 450 billion. In 2013 the EU was the world's biggest importer and biggest exporter of agricultural products. Given its dominant position in world agriculture trade, the EU's policies can have a significant impact on other countries whose economies depend on agriculture.

Table 5.1   Basic agricultural statistics for the EU, 2012

| | EU trade in food and agricultural products | | | Change in food prices (%)* | Expenditure on FBT** as share of total consumer expenditure of households (%) |
	Imports of food and agri products: share of total imports (%)	Exports of food and agri products: share of total exports (%)	Trade balance (Mil EUR)		
UK	8.8	6.2	−24 733.8	3.2	12.7
Sweden	7.8	3.7	−5006.7	1.5	15.6
Finland	7.9	4.2	−2356.3	5.6	17.2
Portugal	13.4	9.9	−2999.5	3.2	20.3
Austria	7.9	7.8	−931.5	3.3	13.4
Netherlands	11.0	15.1	25 877.7	2.0	14.8
Luxembourg	9.0	6.7	−931.8	2.6	16.9
Italy	9.6	8.2	−4367.4	2.6	17.0
Ireland	14.3	16.5	8001.7	0.6	15.8
France	8.4	13.5	15 585.4	2.9	16.6
Spain	9.8	15.0	8741.6	2.1	16.9
Greece	11.9	17.0	−1222.0	1.5	20.6
Germany	8.3	6.0	−9804.2	3.3	14.7
Denmark	12.8	19.2	6585.5	4.3	14.9
Belgium	8.8	9.7	3625.0	3.3	16.9
Romania	8.9	9.3	−728.9	2.2	–
Poland	8.3	11.6	3818.3	4.2	25.3
Bulgaria	9.4	16.6	1009.2	3.2	26.6
EU-27	5.7	6.8	12 220.0	3.0	16.5
USA	4.9	9.7	27 322.5	2.5	–
Japan	7.5	0.4	−49 090.6	–	–

Notes:
*   Change from previous year.
** Food, Beverages and Tobacco.

Sources: European Commission; Eurostat and Directorate-General for Agriculture, FAO and UNSO.

The US is the EU-27's largest single export destination (17 per cent of total exports in 2012) and China is its most significant import source (16 per cent of total imports in 2012). In recent years, China has also been the second fastest growing market after Saudi Arabia for the EU's agricultural exports. The EU is one of the largest agricultural importers from developing countries due to the numerous trade preferences it has granted to former colonies.

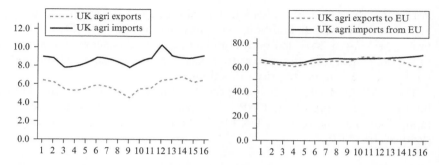

Figure 5.2   Export share of UK agricultural imports and exports: % of total (left panel) and EU share of UK agricultural imports and exports: % of total (right panel)

Agriculture in the UK Economy

Figure 5.2 shows that agricultural trade has stabilized. Both the export and import share of agriculture have been fairly constant, at around 6 per cent and 9 per cent respectively. The EU share of exports has dropped a little to around 60 per cent but the EU import share has remained at around 65 per cent. The UK's balance of trade in agricultural products with EU countries stood at a deficit of EUR 22 billion in 2013 and with non-EU countries at a deficit of EUR 3.7 billion.

Household Consumption and Prices of Food Articles

In the EU-27 countries, spending on food and tobacco account for about 16.5 per cent of consumer spending, the highest shares being in Poland, Bulgaria, Portugal and Greece (Table 5.1). Consumers in the EU tend to pay more for their food than in the US. In the EU, food prices are 17 per cent above world prices, with state support for producers contributing 28 per cent of farm revenues. In comparison, in New Zealand prices are just 2 per cent higher than in the US, with only 1 per cent state support (Niemietz, 2013).

In comparison to the average EU (EU-28) food basket, prices in the UK were 14 per cent higher in 2007 but just 2 per cent higher by 2012. This in part is due to lower VAT rates in the UK as compared to other EU countries.

It has been estimated that consumers of rice in Japan, bananas in Europe and sugar in the US pay as much as two or three times the global price because of agricultural trade distortions. The Common Agriculture

Policy (CAP) of the EU adds substantially to food prices (see section 5.4 below for details). In addition, in recent years the high volatility in food prices, peaking in 2008, led both high-income and low-income countries to impose export restrictions so as to isolate domestic consumers from the food price rises, adding to price distortions.

The CAP (at EUR 55 billion) accounts for 42 per cent of the EU budget. The funding of the CAP is estimated to add £7.65 per week to family food bills and costs the UK £10.3 billion a year, £398 per household (Rotherham, 2010).

5.3   TARIFF BARRIERS

There is little doubt that agricultural protection as evident in high tariff levels remains one of the major distortions in the world economy (see Table 5.2). While in recent years the average tariff on manufactured goods has fallen to 4 per cent in developed countries (4.2 per cent in the EU and 3.3 per cent in the US in 2013), average tariffs on agricultural goods remain above 10 per cent in many developed countries.

As for the US, the average Most Favoured Nation (MFN) rate stood at 4.7 per cent for agri-food products in 2012. The MFN rate is the tariff on imports from member countries of the WTO, unless the country is part of a preferential trade agreement. MFN rates are the highest (most restrictive) that WTO members charge one another. The US agricultural sector also receives a significant portion of government outlays and these outlays nearly doubled between 2004 and 2013.

The 2008 US farm bill, along with other bills passed in July 2012, eliminated the annual fixed direct payments that had been made to farmers

Table 5.2   MFN tariffs across countries on agricultural products

MFN applied	Simple average MFN	Max duty (%)	No. of distinct duty rates	Coefficient of variation
US	4.7	350	770	313
Canada	16.2	551	205	298
EU	13.2	605	1079	127
Japan	16.6	692	323	260
China	15.6	65	46	75

Note: Standard deviation of tariff line duty rates divided by the simple tariff line level average of all duty rates. Includes only *ad valorem* duties or AVEs.

Source: World Tariff report (WTO, ITC, UNCTAD, 2013).

since 1996, and linked protection to specified production of specific crops. Total farm subsidies are expected to decline by 10 per cent over the next ten years (2013–22) with allowance for increased payments in years of low yields or downturns.

The EU MFN tariff on agricultural products is close to 13.2 per cent – more than three times the charges on other goods. While the gap between EU and world prices has fallen over the last decade, the MFN rate still remains relatively high. Furthermore, 90 per cent of subsidized exports notified to the WTO originate from the EU.

In 2013, the average tariff rate was 14.8 per cent for agricultural products as compared to 4.4 per cent for non-agricultural products, and there were 1998 tariff lines. In addition, in comparison to other countries, the maximum duty imposed by the EU on agricultural products is just a little short of double of what it is in the US (Table 5.2). The number of distinct duty rates applied is also one of the highest amongst developed nations in the EU – at 1079 as compared to 323 in Japan.

Overall, tariffs on agricultural products that are not produced in the EU (for example, coffee, tea, spices) are low, but they are higher on primary and processed products. They average 31.7 per cent for dairy products, 25 per cent for sugar refining and 20 per cent for animal products as of 2013.

These estimates do not include the 'snapback' tariffs imposed by the EU when using the special safeguard (SSG) regime of the WTO. An agricultural safeguard clause allows the imposition of supplementary tariffs in the event of import prices falling or import quantities surging relative to specified base-year levels. According to the WTO, the EU has retained the right to use special agricultural safeguard (SSG) arrangements for 539 tariff lines (out of a total of 1998 agricultural tariff lines), although the actual use of this tool has been limited. The price-based SSG has been made operational for chicken, turkey, and sugar products almost continuously, while the EU has calculated trigger volumes for fruit and vegetables on a regular basis.

The EU uses tariff rate quotas (TRQs) – with 114 different TRQs operational in 2009 – which are complex and have highly variable rates. The use of these has grown over time with the enlargement of the EU in order to cater for market access arrangements with the new member states.

Table 5.3 shows how tariff lines are distributed by share of import values. In the EU, 32 per cent of imports are duty free. Of the rest, 25 per cent of imports have 0–10 per cent duties, while 23 per cent have 10–25 per cent duties, as compared to only 7 per cent in the US. Similarly 11 per cent of imports have duties of 25–50 per cent, extremely high compared with other countries in the developed world. This reveals how high protection of agriculture is in the EU compared with other major countries.

*Table 5.3   International comparisons of government policies aimed at
              protecting agriculture*

Agriculture products: Tariff lines and distribution by import value					
Frequency distribution (percent share of imports in each duty category)	Duty-free	0–10%	10–25%	25–50%	50–100%	100% & above
US	30.7	58.5	7.4	1.7	0.3	0.5
Canada	47.8	35	8.9	1.8	1.1	5.3
EU	32.3	25.1	23.4	11.5	4.9	0.8
Japan	36	33.5	18	7	2.1	3.3
China	5.8	33.3	51.4	7	2.5	0

Note: Tariffs are effective rates, i.e. they are a weighted average (by import value) of rates and include an imputed value of subsidies spent on price support.

Source: World Tariff Report (WTO, ITC, UNCTAD, 2013).

In the EU, tariff peaks (triple the simple average) apply to dairy products, beef, cereals and cereal-based products as well as sugar and sweeteners. The range of applied tariffs, in terms of the minimum and maximum rates, is also far wider on agricultural products (from 0 to 605 per cent) than on non-agricultural products (from 0 to 26 per cent). For a given overall tariff average, the greater the dispersion in tariff rates, the greater the likelihood that consumers' and producers' decisions are distorted by the tariff structure. A low average tariff rate could thus disguise significant economic and trade distortions if the dispersion of tariff rates is high. Between 2006 and 2013 the dispersion of tariffs, as measured by the coefficient of variation for primary agriculture and food products, was extremely high. Also the EU's MFN rate for agriculture products according to the WTO stood at 13.2 per cent in 2012 as compared to 4.2 per cent for non-agriculture products.

Even though tariff barriers for agriculture remain high, the agricultural sector also relies heavily on domestic supports. During the ten years to 2009, EU consumers have transferred EUR 1 trillion to agriculture producers (EU). Domestic price supports and export subsidies compound trade distortions, costing taxpayers huge amounts while creating market distortions that spur demand for import protection. The Common Agricultural Policy of the EU is a prime example of such inefficiency.

5.4 THE COMMON AGRICULTURAL POLICY (CAP)

Measures of Protection

The CAP was developed in the early 1960s largely around a price support mechanism which aimed to avoid food shortages by developing a stable internal food market on the basis of a high level of self-sufficiency. The main support to agriculture is through direct payments decoupled from production under the single payment scheme for some states while others follow the single area payment scheme under which each hectare of eligible land qualifies for direct payments. For many commodities, support includes a minimum buying-in price, at which intervention agencies of the member states purchase surplus production; charges are also levied on imported produce so that it enjoys no price advantage over that produced within the EU. The export of products is made possible by the payment of export refunds to enable EU exporters to sell on world markets at the going price. Market support arrangements are financed by the guarantee section of the European Agricultural Guidance and Guarantee Fund (the guidance section of which finances structural measures to promote rural development). Following the introduction of the CAP, the average nominal rate of protection in western Europe increased from 30 per cent in the early 1950s to 40 per cent in the later 1950s, and 60 per cent in the late 1960s (Gulbrandsen and Lindbeck, 1973). In the UK, Ireland and Denmark, levels of agricultural protection were significantly lower before the introduction of the CAP (OECD, 2001b).

Overall, the level of support and protection to agriculture has decreased since the mid-1980s (Table 5.4) and there has been some shift towards less distorting policy measures such as payments based on fixed area, fixed livestock numbers and farm income or receipts. For the OECD area as a whole, the level of support has reduced by nearly half between 1986–88 and 2011–13, while the share of production and trade distorting support has reduced respectively from 95 per cent to 20 per cent and from 86 per cent to 51 per cent.

Nevertheless, the continued significant presence of the most distorting forms of support means that farmers remain shielded from world market signals. Also in the case of the EU, tariff quotas and domestic measures continue to protect specific commodities.

Compared to the levels in the mid-1990s, support to producers, as captured by the Producer Support Estimate (PSE), has fallen across all countries. But it varies widely across countries and commodities. It is an indicator of the annual monetary value of gross transfers from consumers and taxpayers to agricultural producers, measured at the farm gate

Table 5.4 Producer support estimates of support to agriculture (US$ billion)

	2000–02	2011–13	2011	2012	2013p
EU	92.3	83.9	77.9	86.3	87.6
	(35)	(19.2)	(18.3)	(19.6)	(19.8)
US	46.9	31.8	31.0	33.5	31.0
	(21)	(7.6)	(7.6)	(7.9)	(7.4)
Canada	4.3	7.1	7.4	7.8	6.2
	(19)	(13.7)	(14.8)	(14.5)	(11.6)
Japan	47.8	46.8	44.1	48.0	48.3
	(59)	(54.0)	(51.3)	(55.1)	(55.6)

Notes:
Figures in brackets are the percentage PSE, which is the ratio of the PSE to the value of total gross farm receipts, measured by the value of total production (at farm gate prices).
p: provisional estimate.

Source: OECD Producer and Consumer Support Estimates database, 2014.

level, arising from policy measures which support agriculture, regardless of their nature, objectives or impacts on farm production or income. PSE includes market price support, budgetary payments and budget revenue forgone (gross transfers from consumers and taxpayers to agricultural products arising from policy measures based on output, input use, area). Thus it measures protection due to tariffs and tariff quotas, input subsidies, direct payments to producers (both decoupled and coupled to prices or production).

Compared with the 2000–02 period, 2011–13 was characterized by a lower overall level of support to producers, except in Japan and Canada. For Japan, the level of support is lower as compared to 1995–97, with 2000–02 being a period of low PSE. Prices received by OECD farmers in 2013 were on average 18 per cent above world prices. While this is a significant reduction from the mid-1980s when producer prices were 37 per cent higher, farmers in many countries remain shielded from world market signals. Whereas prices received by farmers were 7 per cent higher in the US, farmers in the EU received 20 per cent higher prices. For the EU, the PSE has declined from a peak of EUR 105 billion in 1999 (38 per cent of gross farm receipts) to EUR 87.6 billion in 2013. CAP reforms have contributed to this decline. But in part the rise in international prices has been an important factor which has reduced intervention (OECD, 2014b). As a result, market price support has become a smaller portion of the total support to agriculture over the years, from 50 per cent in 2003 to just 12 per cent in 2011.

The share of support in the form of payments based on area, animals, receipts and income for the OECD countries has increased from 9 per cent of the OECD PSE in 1986–88 to 19 per cent in 1995–97, and to 39 per cent in 2011–13. A major contributor to this change has been the EU, where such payments contributed 60 per cent of the total PSE in 2011–13.

Turning to export subsidies, market-distorting subsidies remain high according to the OECD. Although the share of farmers' income from subsidies declined from 19 per cent in 2012 to 18 per cent in 2013 – almost half of the level seen in the mid-1980s (37 per cent) – the share of support from price and trade-distorting policies still accounted for 51 per cent of the total. In the EU, export subsidies in agriculture have declined but are still being used for commodities such as poultry meat, eggs, beef and veal. Total export refunds amounted to EUR 179 million in 2011 as compared to EUR 1443 million in 2007.

The OECD (2014b) estimates the size of total transfers to the farm sector from taxpayers and consumers as a result of agricultural protection in the OECD, at US$ 258 billion in 2013. The total support estimate (TSE) represents the total policy transfer to the agriculture sector. TSE transfers consist of transfers to agricultural producers (measured by the PSE), consumers (measured by the Consumer Subsidy Equivalent, CSE, support paid to consumers to keep food prices down; it is additional to PSE which is paid to producers) and support to general services to agricultural sector (measured by the General Services Support Estimate (GSSE). TSE as a percentage of GDP for OECD countries as a whole stood at 0.75 per cent in 2013, implying that total transfers for agricultural support policies accounted for 0.75 per cent of OECD countries' total GDP.

In the EU, the total support to the sector (TSE) remains high at EUR 86 billion (2011). This accounts for 0.76 per cent of GDP in 2013, down from 1.44 per cent of GDP in 2000. However, this is slightly above the OECD average and substantially above the US total support estimate of 0.5 per cent of GDP in 2013.

Despite production costs being considerably higher in the EU, it has maintained market share in many agricultural commodities through the CAP's complex range of subsidies. Policies providing support prices, implemented through trade barriers and other export support, or deficiency payments that raise producer revenues to target levels, shield producer returns from world market signals.

The current support levels impose a burden on consumers and taxpayers in the OECD countries. They also constrain agricultural growth and development opportunities in non-OECD countries.

Inter-country Transfers within the EU due to EU Agricultural Protection

The challenge for the EU is to ensure well-functioning markets and implement better targeted measures that are less production and trade distorting. In this section we look at such measures under the CAP and its impact on EU member countries.

The latest budget for the CAP is lower than the previous period (2007–13) at EUR 363 billion over the coming six years in 2011 prices. The latest estimate of the cost of the CAP in the EU stands at EUR 58.8 billion for 2015, a fall of 0.8 per cent from the previous year. This has been supported by reforms undertaken over the past two decades that have reduced the gap between domestic prices and world prices from 33 per cent in 1995–97 to 5 per cent in 2011–13.

As the UK is a net importer of foodstuffs, the impact of the market distortions due to the CAP in the UK is likely to be higher than the average. First, for imports from outside the EU, the tariff and variable levy revenue which would normally accrue to the UK have to be handed over to the EU as part of the EU budget's own resources. Second, for imports from the rest of the EU, the UK must pay the high EU price and thus suffer a terms of trade loss on its imports, compared to the alternative of importing them at world market prices. Thus, the UK is not only paying more for its own food imports as a result of the CAP, but also contributing to the EU agricultural budget to pay for the export subsidies paid to the net exporting EU countries.

Between 2007 and 2013, France was the largest recipient of CAP funding, claiming 15.6 per cent of total budget. The next biggest recipients were Germany (11.5 per cent), Spain (11.0 per cent), and Italy (9.5 per cent) (EC, 2013a). Figure 5.3 shows the percentage which the UK and other member states contributed to this EU funding in 2013, and the amount received back as a percentage of total spending and of total CAP spending.

Between 2007 and 2013, the UK contributed £33.7 billion to the CAP and received £26.6 billion, making a net contribution of £7.1 billion (Howarth et al., 2012). Per hectare, the UK receives £188 compared to France, Germany and the Netherlands, which received £236, £251 and £346 respectively. Germany is the main net contributor, accounting for 21 per cent of financing and only 11 per cent of spending as of 2013. In recent years, since the accession of new countries in the EU, countries such as Poland, Romania and Hungary now account for a significant portion of CAP funding (accounting for close to 16 per cent of CAP funding in 2013) while making a smaller contribution to the EU budget (in total these three countries contribute 5 per cent).

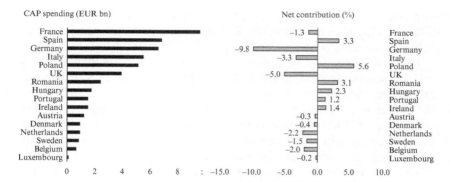

Source: European Union database, Agricultural and Rural Development, The Common Agricultural Policy.

Figure 5.3   Member states' share in EU financing and in spending (% share in EU), 2013

Looking ahead, according to the 2014–20 financial frameworks, these countries are estimated to see a rise in their share of CAP spending. In absolute terms, however, France will remain the largest beneficiary of CAP funding (16 per cent), followed by Germany, Spain and Italy.

Also the addition of newer member states will increase the burden on present members, reducing their share in CAP spending while their contribution to the EU budget will remain significant.

CAP and its Reform Process

In this section we turn to the history of the CAP and how it has evolved into its present form. Reforms to the CAP to curb over-production were introduced in 1984, 1988 and, most radically, in 1992. These involved a market-oriented price strategy (the resulting drop in agricultural incomes being cushioned by specific income support); quantitative and qualitative control of production through quotas and compensatory payments; premiums for set-aside schemes (grants to farmers to take land out of production); and diversification of production to bring supply more in line with demand.

One of the most important reforms in the CAP were the MacSharry reforms of 1992. The core of the reforms was a nominal cut of 30 per cent in the cereal price, phased over three years, complemented by a smaller cut in the institutional prices for beef and butter. These price cuts were compensated by payments per tonne, translated on the basis of regional yields to a per hectare payment. In reality, the implementation of the 1992 reforms resulted in a substantial over-compensation of cereal prices, estimated at EUR 8.5 billion over the four years from 1994 to 1997. The CAP reforms also penalized efficient producers since the compensatory subsidies are based on an average yield.

Johnson (1995) and Messerlin (2001) confirm that although the 1992 reforms represented a significant change in the structure of farm support in Europe, they did not reduce the level of support and thus failed to reduce the welfare cost of agricultural protection. Since the MacSharry reforms, the EU has continued to pursue a strategy of agricultural exports by a combination of export subsidies, internal price support, and direct aid to producers to compensate for revenue losses.

The next important step in the reform process came as the 'Agenda 2000', agreed in Berlin in March 1999. These changes, however, did not seize the opportunity to reform the milk quota or sugar quota regimes, with extensions adopted instead. Pressures to adapt the CAP to new requirements arose from enlargement, where the Commission had proposed a progressive introduction of direct payments.

Further CAP reforms in July 2003 also failed in several respects. First, according to an agreement reached between France and Germany, there was no change in the size of the CAP budget, which at EUR 50 billion (US$ 58 billion) a year continued to take up nearly half of all EU spending. Second, cereal prices, which the Commission had proposed should be cut by 5 per cent, remained unchanged. The EU also failed to cut the link between subsidy and production. One of the most damaging features of the CAP was that the money was tied to production, with surpluses dumped on world markets via the payment of export subsidies.

The new Common Agricultural Policy for 2014–20 retains the two pillars of support, direct payments and market-related expenditure (pillar 1) and rural development (pillar 2), but increases the links between them. It moves from product to producer support and now to a more land-based approach. It also entails more flexibility to implement policies at the national level with the possibility to transfer 15 per cent of the amount between the two pillars mentioned above. However, the latter provides room for member states to reintroduce commodity specific and output-linked measures.

In real terms the CAP funding for 2014–20 is lower than the previous period at EUR 362 billion (at 2011 prices) with EUR 277 billion for direct payments and market-related expenditure (Pillar 1) and EUR 84.9 billion for rural development (pillar 2). The shift in CAP reforms over the years is most starkly visible in the drop of expenditure spent on market management – from 90 per cent of total CAP expenditure (driven by export refunds and intervention purchases) in 1992 to only 5 per cent as market intervention in 2013. The major source of payments has now become direct payments, of which 94 per cent are decoupled from production.

5.5 WELFARE COSTS

In this section we discuss the cost of agricultural protection to the world economy in general and the EU in particular. Many studies have used analytical techniques to show that the benefits of agricultural protection which accrue to producers in that sector are offset by higher prices as well as lower production and income elsewhere in the economy.

A study by CEPII (Decreux and Fontagné, 2011) shows that benefits arising from the Doha Development Agenda (DDA) negotiations in WTO could increase world exports by US$ 359 billion on an annual basis from a deal on the liberalization of industrial goods, agriculture and services. This would translate into 0.2 per cent of additional world economic growth and an extra US$ 30 billion in GDP for the EU. A sizeable portion of welfare gains from cutting agricultural intervention would accrue to the EU (US$ 9.8 billion) and Australia and New Zealand (US$ 8.3 billion). Bouët and Laborde (2009) find that following the conclusion of the Doha Round in July 2008, world exports would grow by 1.46 per cent in 2025 or US$ 336 billion, compared to the situation without agreement. World GDP would grow by 0.09 per cent, adding US$ 59 billion from 2025 onwards.

Kerkela et al. (2005) analyse the impact of removing agricultural export subsidies by the EU using a multi-region and multi-sector general equilibrium model (GTAP). Reducing export subsidies would increase EU GDP by 0.03 per cent. In aggregate the welfare gain is the most for EU but is also positive for Australia and New Zealand, which would benefit from the increasing prices and markets for their exportable agriculture products.

In addition to the studies discussed above, which estimate the welfare cost of agricultural protection to the world economy, there are several studies which focus on the cost of agricultural protection in the EU. Using a partial equilibrium model, the EU (2000) estimated that full implementation of a reduction in support prices for cereals, beef and dairy products under Agenda 2000 CAP reforms would result in an increase in consumer welfare of EUR 8.8 billion in 2005/06 and EUR 10.5 billion in 2006/07. The simulation results of Borrell and Hubbart (2000) based on the GTAP model suggest that the CAP has made the non-grain sector eight times larger than it would otherwise be and has enlarged the milk products and grains sectors by more than 50 per cent. The study also confirms that without the CAP the EU would greatly increase its agricultural imports and decrease imports of other products because non-agricultural sectors would expand. The scrapping of the CAP would increase US and Canadian exports of dairy products by over 70 per cent and of crops by between 25 and 46 per cent. The dairy and meat sectors in Australia and

New Zealand would expand. The total welfare cost of the CAP to the EU is estimated at 0.9 per cent of GDP. The costs imposed on Australia, New Zealand, Latin America and the rest of the world are also substantial. These results may underestimate the welfare cost because they do not take into account dynamic gains from higher capital accumulation and the productivity boost that would occur as a result of open competitive markets. The results from Stoeckel and Breckling (1989) suggest that omitting these factors could underestimate the costs by at least 20 per cent.

The Danish Research Institute of Food Economics (2013) examines the economy-wide effects of full decoupling (a uniform land payment) measured against a baseline of 1997–2013. Using the GTAP general equilibrium model, the study estimates that the EU would gain welfare benefits of EUR 10.5 billion in 2013 (0.06 per cent of GDP), with the UK gaining some EUR 3.4 billion (0.04 per cent of GDP) as a result of the move towards decoupling payments.[1] The overwhelming majority of the welfare gains would be achieved through a more efficient allocation of resources. That the UK's share of the benefits is so large reflects the comparative advantage of other sectors of the UK economy relative to agriculture. Changes in production are estimated in the model: EU wheat production falls by 7 per cent, other grains by 6 per cent, oilseeds by 9 per cent and beef and veal by 11 per cent; fruit and vegetable production rises by 2 per cent. Other sectors of the economy would see an increase in production in the region of 0.2 per cent. The value of the subsidy is capitalized into significantly higher land prices. The analysis assumes that decoupling would be largely budget-neutral but there is no breakdown of the welfare gains between consumers and producers.

As the above evidence suggests, the costs of trade protection in agriculture and the benefits of trade liberalization are well established. Beyond the direct observable cost, agricultural support policies pursued in the EU have caused distortions in the allocation of resources. Higher domestic prices have given incentives to retain more resources – land, labour and capital – in agriculture than would have been the case if farmers had faced world market prices. Logically, it should be in the EU's own interest to reform agricultural protection as quickly as possible. However, agricultural trade reforms in the EU have been slow. There has been resistance to liberalization by those who would stand to lose and the sector is viewed as being fundamentally different from other sectors due to issues related to environmental protection, food security, and preservation of the landscape.

EU enlargement is another issue that is likely to raise costs of the CAP. Currently the EU is in the process of including nine south-eastern countries in the union, whose agricultural share of GDP is well above the EU 2012 average of 1.7 per cent, ranging from 7.4 per cent in Bosnia and Herzegovina to 20.6 per cent in Albania. Therefore applying the CAP to these countries would result in a considerable rise in expenditure while given their low per capita income and GDP level, their contribution to the overall EU budget will be less.

This would also imply a greater burden on existing EU members such as the UK. Looking at past data, the last accession round in 2004 and 2007 brought 12 new countries into the EU (Cyprus, Czech Republic, Estonia, Hungary, Latvia, Lithuania, Malta, Poland, Slovakia, Slovenia, Bulgaria and Romania). These countries account for 23 per cent of the total CAP spending in the EU as of 2013, up from 12 per cent in 2007.

5.6   EU'S AGRICULTURAL TRADE DISPUTES

Most of the disputes under the WTO/GATT between the EU and the US in the early 1980s were about trade in agricultural products. Nearly 90 per cent of all US actions against the EU involved agriculture. In fact, three-quarters of all lawsuits by any country against the EU involved agricultural products. By contrast, only roughly 40 per cent of all lawsuits against the US covered agriculture, and these were mostly actions brought by the EU. The US was initially concerned with the shrinking market in Europe, as trade diversion took place encouraged by the high trade barriers after the introduction of the single market. Then the issue changed to the use of export subsidies as the EU tried to keep surpluses from depressing the internal market. In the 1980s there were major differences between the EU and the US over what constitutes a subsidy and over how to determine the magnitude of subsidies. The US retaliated against EU subsidies with its Export Enhancement Program (EEP), expressly targeted at those markets where the EU was increasing its share.

The 1990s once again witnessed a sharp intensification of trade disputes between the EU and the US. The main agricultural trade disputes between the US and the EU are: (1) the beef hormone dispute; (2) the banana dispute; (3) the bans as a result of BSE; (4) problems due to foot and mouth disease; and (5) genetically modified organisms (GMOs).

In 1989, the EU banned the use of six growth hormones used for cattle and prohibited the imports of beef containing such hormones. The ban led to a GATT lawsuit, and later to a WTO dispute settlement case filed in 1996 by the US and other beef-exporting nations. The ruling was in the US's favour. In view of the non-compliance by the EC with the WTO ruling, the Dispute Settlement Body authorized the US in 1999 to impose retaliatory tariffs on imports from the EC of US$ 117 million per year. The measure is still active.

In 1993, following the implementation of the Single Market, the EU imposed an EU-wide system of import quotas for bananas. The new system led to two GATT lawsuits, and later to two WTO dispute settlement cases filed in 1995 and 1996 by the US and several Latin American countries. This dispute was also solved in favour of the US. In 1999, the US imposed retaliatory tariffs on imports from the EC of US$ 191 million per year. The measure was deactivated in 2001, but US$ 116 million in punitive duties remains in effect due to the beef dispute. This, in turn, led the EU to threaten retaliation against US$ 4 billion in US exports that the WTO found in violation of an export subsidy agreement. In addition, the EU has filed numerous WTO dispute resolution petitions alleging that a variety of US trade laws violate international obligations in some technical fashion.

In the early 2000s some of the most contentious EU–US agricultural trade issues were in the area of Sanitary and Phytosanitary Standards (SPS) and other more technical trade issues. These include the dispute over the import of hormone-treated beef into Europe, the potential ban by Europe of imports of beef by-products ('specified risk materials') that may harbour vectors of bovine spongiform encephalopathy (BSE, or mad cow disease) and that over the regulation of the use and labelling of genetically modified organisms (GMOs).

More recently the EU is demanding that the US recognize and protect the EU's list of geographical indications (GIs) – defined as indications which identify a good as originating in the territory of a member state. This is important for the EU as it is unlikely to be competitive in the production of basic agricultural commodities, but production of commodities linked to its heritage are valued by consumers. As of 2010, the European commission estimated the value of GI products at EUR 54.3 billion – close to 6 per cent of the output of the EU food and drink industry.

The Russian ban on the imports of some food products from the EU has also resulted in demand for compensation and aid by certain member states. The Russian market is the second most important agri-food market for the EU after the US, with an export share of 10 per cent. The European Commission can use the crisis reserve fund to support member countries in this situation. The reserve fund amounting to EUR 425 billion is created by reducing direct payments made to farmers, thus acting as a brake on any rent-seeking behaviour by the member states.

NOTE

1. The key change in recent EU reform proposals is 'decoupling' or separating payments from production. This means that farmers will still receive money, at a level based on past income, but it will be in the form of a one-off payment that hopefully encourages them to farm for the market, rather than subsidies.

6.   Manufacturing

The importance of the manufacturing industry across the world has increased since the financial crisis of 2008. Manufacturing is seen as a prime job-creating sector and for this reason one might expect that the protection of manufactured goods in the EU and the rest of the world will begin to gain importance as countries make an effort to boost the domestic manufacturing sector. Certain labour-intensive sectors such as textiles already continue to be relatively highly protected by both tariff and non-tariff barriers globally. This chapter analyses the issues surrounding the impact of the EU's trade barriers in industrial products and overall trends in the manufacturing sector.

The first section considers the structural shift within the manufacturing sector in developed countries and the growing importance of technology-driven industries. It discusses the significance of manufacturing for output and employment in the EU and other industrial nations. The second section reviews the data on trade in manufacturing goods. Section 3 describes the level and evolution of barriers to trade in goods in the EU and the US in recent years. Section 4 presents estimates of trade barriers which take into account both tariff and non-tariff barriers. Section 5 outlines the main empirical findings on the welfare effects of trade liberalization.

6.1   ROLE OF THE MANUFACTURING SECTOR IN GDP AND EMPLOYMENT

In the European Union, the importance of the manufacturing sector has re-emerged since the financial crisis. Countries with a strong manufacturing base, rather than those that were heavily dependent on services, were seen to fare better during and after the crisis – for example Germany. The European Commission (2010) highlighted that 'a vibrant and highly competitive EU manufacturing sector is essential for a more sustainable, inclusive and resource-efficient economy'. This increased focus on manufacturing has raised concerns over the decline in manufacturing production in some member states.

Over the last two decades the share of industrial production in GDP has

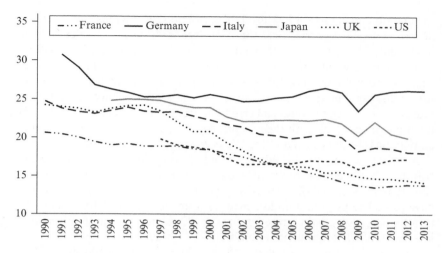

Source: OECD (2012).

Figure 6.1   Industry as a percentage of GDP

continuously declined in the US and the EU Member States (Figure 6.1). UK industrial output as a proportion of GDP fell from 32 per cent in 1970 to 14 per cent by 2013. In the same period it declined from 25 per cent to 17 per cent in the US and it fell from 36 per cent to 26 per cent in Germany.

A similar pattern is noted for the manufacturing sector, a subset of industrial output. The value-added share of manufacturing in the EU has dropped from 19 per cent in 2000 to 16 per cent as of 2013 – much lower than the 20 per cent target by the EU for 2020. The manufacturing sector accounts for 14 per cent of total employment, 67 per cent of exports and 65 per cent of private R&D in the EU.

While the overall manufacturing share in GDP has fallen, some sectors have gained in importance. In the UK over the last decade, the chemical (including pharmaceutical), electrical and optical sectors – which include IT and communications – have all grown faster than the economy as a whole. Certain industries, such as basic steel, textiles and clothing, and shipbuilding, suffered from their competitive advantage moving to less developed countries and experienced a decline in manufacturing capacity and employment that was not subsequently reversed. In the US, leading industries include motor vehicles, aerospace, telecommunications, chemicals, electronics and computers.

As the share of manufacturing in total output has tended to decline across all the leading economies, the proportion of workers employed in the manufacturing sector has also fallen. Manufacturing jobs have declined in most OECD countries over the past decade. In Germany, they fell by 5 per cent, while in the UK they fell by over 25 per cent and in the US by 20 per cent between 2000 and 2008. During this period, certain countries such as Luxembourg, Poland, Estonia, Austria and Italy have seen a rise in employment in the manufacturing sector as firms have relocated to reduce costs. Since the financial crisis, the EU has experienced record high unemployment rates, with the exception of Germany, as overall economic activity has slowed down and the EU economy remains fragile.

Another reason for the fall in manufacturing employment in OECD countries has been that production has become more capital intensive and skills based. Most labour-intensive jobs such as assembly and packaging have moved to poor and middle income countries. In the future any addition to jobs may remain limited in the OECD economies but highly skilled job creation will continue in manufacturing as well as related services.

UK manufacturing accounted for 8 per cent of the total workforce in 2009 compared to 14 per cent in the early 2000s. In 2009, the four major industries were food, beverages and tobacco, publishing and printing, fabricated metals and chemicals and pharmaceuticals; these accounted for 46 per cent of gross value added and 43 per cent of employment in the sector.

The characteristics of the UK manufacturing sector have changed over time and like other leading manufacturing countries such as Germany, Japan and the US, the UK has specialized in higher technology industries such as aerospace. Figure 6.2 shows the growth in higher technology industries while lower-tech industries have contracted between 1994 and 2009.

In the EU, the productivity growth performance of the manufacturing sector has been the weakest in Italy and Spain and the strongest in Sweden, Finland and Ireland. In Finland, productivity growth in manufacturing has outperformed that in services by a factor of six. In Germany, the productivity growth rate of manufacturing is three times that of services. In UK, the growth in total factor productivity (TFP) in manufacturing has been at 2.3 per cent per year between 1980 and 2009 as compared to 0.7 per cent per year for the UK economy as a whole (Government Office for Science, 2013).

Skill sets play an important role in increasing productivity. In the UK, the education level of the manufacturing workforce has doubled over time, with 17 per cent holding a degree in 2009 as compared to only 9.4 per cent in 1994. This increase has partly come from a shift towards more high-skilled occupations such as product and support services, research and development, and sales and marketing professionals. Educational attainment in these categories is high: close to 31 per cent of these employees held a degree in 2009. In comparison to its main competitors like Germany,

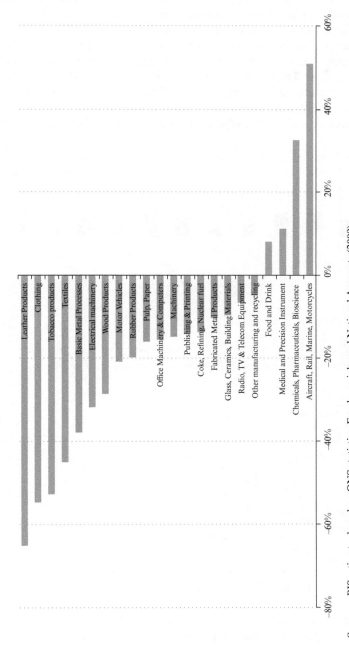

Source: BIS estimates based on ONS statistics, Employee jobs and National Accounts (2009).

Figure 6.2 UK manufacturing sector percentage growth or contraction in real value added, 1994–2009

China, France and Japan, it lags behind in skill levels, but it is ahead of the US. This can be seen in Figure 6.3, which shows the percentage of employees in manufacturing with science and engineering degrees in 2006.

The manufacturing and services nexus has increased in the EU in the last two decades. A large share of value added in the manufacturing output comes from services. The service intensity – measured as the share of services in manufacturing output – increased to 22 per cent in 1995 and further to 24 per cent by 2009 (see Figure 6.4).

This 'servicetization' of manufacturing is also seen in the employment

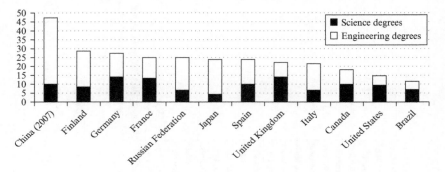

Source: OECD, STAN Database (2006).

Figure 6.3   *Percentage of employees in manufacturing with science and engineering degrees at first-stage university level, 2006*

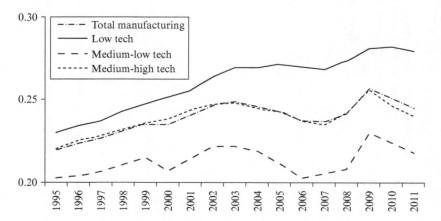

Figure 6.4   *Service inputs into the manufacturing sector relative to manufacturing gross output for the EU-27, 1995–2011*

shift in manufacturing. In the UK, manufacturing employment has shifted away from production sales towards professional support services, logistics and distribution, sales and marketing, and research and development activities (BIS analysis based on ONS Labor force survey data).

6.2 TRADE IN INDUSTRIAL GOODS: THE EUROPEAN UNION

Recently, global trade has been slow to pick up with merchandise trade, growing at just 2 per cent globally in volume between 2012 and 2013 due to slow output growth. However, this is in contrast with the performance of trade in the past. In the last two decades, the global trade landscape has undergone a shift. As a share of global output, trade is now at almost three times its share in the early 1950s despite the dip after the crisis. Most of this rise has come from growth in high-technology products such as computers and electronics, with their share rising to more than 20 per cent of global GDP in 2008. The regional dynamics show that growth in trade has been the strongest for Europe and Asia.

Manufacturing accounts for three-quarters of total goods exports from Europe. Exports are more concentrated towards processed goods while imports are mostly energy and raw materials goods. The EU's economy is relatively open in comparison to those of the US, China and Japan. Its trade openness has increased since 1998, primarily due to growing trade between new EU Member States and China. As of 2012, exports of goods to non-EU countries accounted for almost 39 per cent of GDP, up from 25 per cent in 1999. By 2008–12, trade of the EU with the rest of the world accounted for 40 per cent of total exports and 43 per cent of total imports.

The US is the EU's largest single trading partner, accounting for a 12 per cent share of total exports from the region between 2008 and 2012. The importance of China as a trading partner has risen in the last decade. Its share in total EU imports has risen from 9.6 per cent (2003–07) to 12.3 per cent between 2008 and 2012. This is followed by Russia at 7.5 per cent.

Trade within EU countries accounts for close to 32 per cent of total exports and 27 per cent of total imports. Amongst EU countries, the UK is the largest trading partner of the euro area, accounting for 13 per cent of EU exports and 10 per cent of EU imports. Looking at the sectoral composition of extra-euro area imports and exports, imports have a higher share of energy and raw materials, while exports are more biased towards processed goods. In euro-zone exports, machinery and transport equipment account for 40 per cent of total trade in goods, other manufactured articles for 23.6 per cent, chemicals for 16 per cent and food, drink and tobacco account for 7 per cent.

The revealed comparative advantage (RCA) indicator for the EU shows that the region has a comparative advantage in two-thirds of its industrial sectors. In 2011, the RCA was high in printing, beverages, tobacco and products, and pharmaceuticals, while in sectors such as computer, electronic and optical products, textiles, other manufacturing, clothing, and refined petroleum the RCA was lower than 0.8. At the country level, Cyprus, Greece, Luxembourg, Lithuania, the Netherlands, Poland and Romania are more specialized in tobacco products in 2011. Ireland and Belgium have high RCAs in the production of pharmaceuticals and Portugal and Italy and Romania are specialized in leather and footwear.

Comparative advantage is also classified according to technological intensities. Trade performance based on technological intensities show that Cyprus, Hungary, Ireland and Malta have the highest comparative advantage in high technology products. Overall, the EU-27 has a comparative advantage in medium technology products of 1.14 but lags behind the US (1.22) and Japan (1.59) in this category. The UK has a comparative advantage in high and medium high technology products. The share of high technology exports as a percentage of total manufactured exports was in 2012 higher in the UK (21.7 per cent) as compared with Germany (15.8 per cent) and the United States (see Table 6.1). This partly reflects the UK's strength, vis-à-vis other countries, in pharmaceuticals and aerospace, and these two industries appear to be strongly placed in world markets.

The IT hardware sector, including computers and communication equipment, is also a strong performer; exports of these products, as a proportion of total exports of manufactures, is higher in the UK than in

Table 6.1   High technology exports as a percentage of total manufactured exports

	2005	2006	2007	2008	2009	2010	2011	2012
China	30.8	30.5	26.7	25.6	27.5	27.5	25.8	26.3
France	20.3	21.5	18.5	20.0	22.6	24.9	23.7	25.4
Germany	17.4	17.1	14.0	13.3	15.3	15.3	15.0	15.8
Japan	23.0	22.1	18.4	17.3	18.8	18.0	17.5	17.4
Russian Federation	8.4	7.8	6.9	6.5	9.2	9.1	8.0	8.4
Spain	7.3	6.4	5.1	5.3	6.2	6.4	6.5	7.0
United Kingdom	28.4	33.0	19.4	18.1	23.2	20.9	21.3	21.7
United States	29.9	30.1	27.2	25.9	21.5	19.9	18.1	17.8

Source: World Bank, World Development Indicators.

Germany or France. Most of these exports derive from foreign-owned companies, which are also large importers.

Trade Development: United States

The US is the largest exporter of merchandise in the world, second to China. Export growth in the US has been above the average of the advanced world and is expected to continue along this trend in the coming years. In 2013, goods trade was at US$ 3.8 trillion, with manufactured goods accounting for 87 per cent of total exports and 81 per cent of total imports. Canada is the largest US export market, accounting for 19 per cent of US exports. This share has, however, declined since 1999, when it was 24 per cent. The EU is the next most important export destination for the US, accounting for 17 per cent of its exports – down from 22 per cent in 1999. China's share has increased fourfold from 2 per cent in 1999 to 8 per cent in 2013. The share of OPEC countries has also increased to 5 per cent from 3 per cent in 1999, and that of South and Central America has risen to 12 per cent from 8 per cent during the same period.

US imports stood at US$ 2.3 trillion in 2013 as compared to US$ 1.0 trillion in 1999. In the wake of the financial crisis and weak domestic demand, import growth has slowed to 1.4 per cent in the last five years (2008–13) as compared to 6.6 per cent between 2000 and 2005. The highest share of imports comes from China – close to 19 per cent in 2013. This share has risen dramatically from 8 per cent in 1999. China has taken over from Canada and the European Union, each of whose 19 per cent share in imports in 1999 has now fallen to 15 per cent and 17 per cent respectively in 2013. The share of South and Central America has remained constant at around 7 per cent in the last decade. Elsewhere, OPEC countries account for a 7 per cent share of US imports in 2013, up from 4 per cent in 1999.

6.3   BARRIERS TO TRADE IN GOODS

Since the Second World War, global and regional trade patterns have been influenced first by trade liberalization, then by vertical specialization and income convergence. In developed countries such as Europe and the US, trade barriers have come down from 15 per cent in 1952 to 4 per cent in 2005. A major part of this decline took place during the 1950s and 1960s (WTO). Tariffs were high in many countries until the 1980s but since then have come down considerably.

Tariffs

After the successive tariff cuts during the various GATT rounds, average MFN tariffs on manufactures are rather low, with the US and the EU both among the low-tariff regions. If we consider non-weighted tariff averages, the US and the EU each presently apply an average import tariff in the vicinity of no more 5 per cent (World Bank). The average tariff on non-agricultural products (WTO definition, excluding petroleum) in the EU was 4.2 per cent in 2013, down from 4.5 per cent in 1999, and in the US it stands at 3.1 per cent in 2013. The average MFN tariff in manufacturing is 6.5 per cent as of 2013, down from 6.7 per cent in 2008.

Despite these advances in market access in industrial products, there remain a number of issues that are still worth investigating. Many developed countries continue to levy higher tariffs on consumer goods than on capital goods.

In the EU, for example, tariffs on consumer goods such as textiles (6.6 per cent) are more than double those on capital goods such as electrical machinery (2.8 per cent). For clothing the average MFN rate is 11.5 per cent, similar to rates for agriculture products, which have high barriers to trade (fruits, vegetables and plants have an average MFN rate of 10.7 per cent).

According to region, in non-agricultural products, duty free exports from the EU to China are as low as 9.6 per cent as compared to 50 per cent for Japan and 46 per cent for the US. This implies that China is more restrictive to EU exports than it is for Japanese and US exports. This seems to reflect the EU's policy on non-tariff barriers towards China.

The structure of tariffs in terms of stage of processing continues to show evidence of tariff escalation for the EU at the final stage in 2013, notably for food, beverage and tobacco products, as well as textile products. While in the first stage of processing, simple average MFN rates are close to 6.8 per cent and drop to 4.9 per cent for semi-processed products, they rise to 7.3 per cent for fully processed products.

In July 2002 the US announced a proposal to eliminate all tariffs on consumer and industrial goods worldwide by 2015. However, despite the substantial tariff reduction and elimination agreed in the Uruguay Round by the US, a number of significant duties and tariff peaks remain in various sectors including footwear, textiles and clothing, hides and skins, chemicals, plastic or rubber and stone and glass.

In sum, although average tariff rates have fallen in recent years, tariff peaks and tariff dispersion as measured by their standard deviation and the spread of minimum and maximum rates remain significant in the EU (Table 6.2). The EU average tariffs by ISIC sectors vary widely, mirroring

Table 6.2   Imports and tariff peaks, 2013 (%)

	USA	EU	Japan	Canada
Share of tariff peak products (MFN tariff > 15%)				
All products	2.7	5.1	3.7	6.8
Agricultural products	5.7	26.3	21.8	9.5
Industrial products	2.2	1.6	0.7	6.3
All products				
Maximum duty %	350	511	736	484
Average MFN rate %	3.4	5.5	4.9	4.2
Non-agricultural products				
Average MFN %	3.1	4.2	2.6	2.3
Number of distinct duty rates	9769	111	199	36

Source: WTO (2014).

the existence of very different maximum tariffs. In some cases such as chemicals, the maximum tariff even increased after 1995 as a result of specific tariffs. In the EU, tariff peaks occur in footwear and automotive industries. In the US and Canada, most peaks are in textiles and clothing, footwear, glass and glassware, and electrical parts.

The case of textiles
In the last decade, the EU's textile and clothing industry has undergone a fundamental change, with exports doubling during this period. Since 2009, trade in this sector has become completely quota and licence free. Also the industry has moved towards high end products. In the past the main market for this industry was the EU itself but with the financial crisis and weak demand, the industry has reoriented itself towards emerging economies (EU, 2011).

The EU has long maintained restrictions on imports of textile and clothing products from a number of developing countries and transition economies. Tariffs well above the average apply to textiles and clothing products, with articles of apparel and clothing having average tariff rates close to 6.6 per cent, with a tariff range of 0–12 per cent.

Non-Tariff Barriers (NTB)

Quantitative restrictions
As tariffs are lowered, other impediments to trade become more apparent. The tariff estimates presented above leave out trade impediments arising out

of non-tariff barriers such as quantitative restrictions and anti-dumping duties, as well as barriers due to labour and environment standards.

The EU does not apply quantitative restrictions to imports from WTO members and countries with which it has bilateral agreements. Therefore, with Russia included in the WTO, quotas on steel products were removed in 2012. Import quotas are applied on certain steel products from Kazakhstan and certain textiles from Belarus and Korea. With Serbia, the EU has a bilateral agreement on trade in textiles, which allows for the possible enforcement of quantitative restrictions on imports of textile products. This agreement will lapse once the Stabilization and Association Agreement between the EU and Serbia comes into force.

The EU continues to maintain restrictions on the basis of security, technical, environmental and sanitary grounds.

Anti-dumping (AD) duties

During the period between 1990 and 1999, quantitative restrictions and AD duties tended to be concentrated in the same sectors. The decline in the former during this period was often compensated for by an expansion of AD measures, in particular in consumer electronics and textiles as well as fisheries and mining.

The general prevalence of, or the perceived likelihood of getting caught in, anti-dumping disputes might also be acting as a permanent trade restriction. As tariffs are reduced or eliminated, and quotas on agricultural products and textile and apparel products are phased out, AD/countervailing duties (CVD) laws are poised to become the most significant trade barrier for reducing import competition from more efficient foreign competitors. The average duration of AD measures in the EU is seven years, with 17 per cent remaining in place for more than ten years.

In 2002, the EU had in place definitive anti-dumping measures (duties and/or undertakings) on 175 product categories, down from 192 in 1999. In 2012, the number of AD measures was 112, affecting 20 trading partners. Between 2008 and 2012 the EU initiated 30 new AD investigations – the same as the number of investigations in the previous five years.

In the last two decades, 14 anti-dumping measures that were longer than ten years old affecting 13 trading partners were terminated or expired. For example, the AD measures on imports of potassium chloride from Belarus and Russia which were imposed in 1992 were terminated in July 2011. Also the AD measures on imports of polyethylene terephthalate from Taiwan, India, Indonesia, Korea, Malaysia and Thailand expired in February 2012.

The EU is the second most frequent user of these measures, behind the US. Although some 40 per cent of the anti-dumping investigations initiated by the EU are terminated without measures being taken, this does not mean that trade is not influenced due to AD initiations. The prospect of protection imposes additional costs on the domestic economy. The mere presence of an AD threat can affect the behaviour of firms and hence market outcomes, even if AD duties are never imposed.

Both domestic and foreign firms alter their profit-maximizing behaviour in order to influence the outcome of potential AD investigations (Blonigen and Prusa, 2001, 2003). The fact that measures may not ultimately be imposed does not alter the fact that the exporter will have had to face considerable disruption to its trade, as well as the time and expense of defending itself even if the case is terminated without measures. Most ironically, the exporters may in most cases raise prices in order to avoid an AD duty. This effectively transfers AD revenue to the foreign firm via a cartel-style benefit.

Over the years certain broad patterns have emerged in terms of the countries being targeted by the EU. For periods during the early 1980s the countries of Central and Eastern Europe were generally the most frequently targeted. During the mid- to late 1980s these were to a large extent replaced by Asian countries, initially Japan and then, in turn, South Korea, Thailand, Indonesia, Malaysia and so on. Indeed, over the six-year period of 1993–98, China was the major target of EU anti-dumping cases, with 26, followed by India (22), Korea (17) and Thailand (14). In 2001 China was the most affected at the end of 2001, with 34 cases, followed by Thailand with 13 cases.

More recently, a majority of AD measures were on imports from Asia, in particular China (see Figure 6.5). Between 2008 and 2012, 74 per cent of the AD measures were imposed on Asia, with other European countries outside the EU accounting for 17 per cent of the AD measures.

Such trends are perhaps not surprising. While there are a number of factors determining who is targeted (and of course the European Commission can essentially only respond to a complaint from the domestic industry), it is clear that these country trends largely reflect the current sources of strong import competition in the types of industries which are likely to be suffering enough injury to warrant an anti-dumping complaint.

In 1998 the most affected product categories were iron and steel products, consumer electronics and chemicals. The number of initiations of new investigations in 1999 rose threefold to 66 and included items such as compact disc boxes and colour-television picture tubes. The EU also had 16 definitive countervailing measures in place, up from 6 in 1999, with products from India the most frequently affected. Safeguard action was taken in March 2002 on 15 steel products in response to the US' safeguard action on steel imports. Supplementary duties are to be triggered by volumes rising above 2001 levels to prevent diversion of trade from the US market onto the EU market.

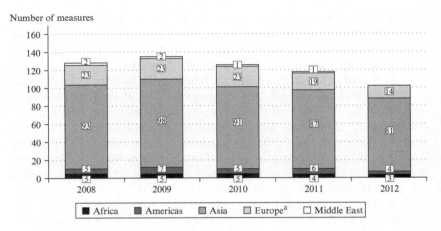

Number of measures

Note: a Other European countries outside the EU.

Source: WTO (2008–12).

Figure 6.5   EU anti-dumping measures in force by region, 2008–12

The Commission also proposed that the Council should agree additional duties of between 8 per cent and 100 per cent on imported products from the US as 're-balancing' measures, given the failure of the two parties to agree compensation for the Article XIX measure on steel imposed by the US. The EU continues to make frequent use of the special safeguard (SSG) mechanism under the WTO Agreement on Agriculture to impose 'snap-back' tariffs.

Between 2008 and 2012, chemical and other metals accounted for 22 per cent of the AD measures imposed by the EU, followed by iron and steel at 20 per cent and mechanical engineering at 10 per cent (Figure 6.6).

The highest AD duties from original investigations between 2010 and 2012 were from India (synthetic fibre ropes) at 82 per cent, from Korea (polyethylene terephthalate) at 143 per cent, and from China (stainless steel seamless pipes and tubes) at 71.9 per cent. Out of all anti-dumping duties, Vietnam faces the highest duty at 707 per cent for stainless steel fasteners imports to the EU.

Technical regulations and state aid
The EU and its member states have adopted technical regulations and conformity assessment procedures. These have been harmonized at the EU level but certain member states have non-harmonized requirements that impede the movement of goods. The EU notified 154 technical regulations

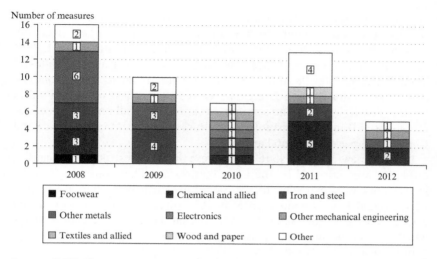

Number of measures

Source: WTO, European Commission (2008–12).

Figure 6.6 EU anti-dumping measures imposed by products, 2008–12

and conformity assessment procedures to the WTO between January 2011 and February 2013. These included electric and electronic equipment, household appliances, machinery, motor vehicle parts, chemicals, food, and textile products. Member states notified 97 regulations, with France accounting for the largest share (25 per cent), followed by the Czech Republic (22 per cent), Sweden (18 per cent), Denmark (6 per cent) and Lithuania (5 per cent). WTO members have been concerned that these regulations and standards would lead to obstacles to trade for foreign small and medium sized firms.

The EU notified 51 regular and 7 emergency sanitary and phytosanitary standard measures to the WTO between 2011 and 2013. Certain WTO members have raised concerns over some EU measures. For example, India raised concern over the testing of pesticide residues in 2012 and China raised concern over the limits on aluminium in floors in 2012.

State aid is another way, though not always visible, to protect domestic industries. As of 2010, the largest two portions of the budget go into expenditure on agriculture and structural and cohesion funds. The total outlays were close to EUR 49 billion in 2010. Over the period of 2007–13, the total allocation amounted to EUR 347 billion. Out of this, EUR 55 billion was for competitiveness and employment. In addition, the European Globalisation Adjustment Fund (EGF) was started in 2007 to support workers that are made redundant due to globalization and the global financial crisis. The workers that received aid belonged to sectors such as basic metals, manufacturing (automotive, textiles) and construction.

Non-crisis aid has been close to EUR 73 billion in 2010 and EUR 64 billion in 2011. Fourteen states have seen a rise in their average state-aid levels between 2006–08 and 2009–11. In comparison to their economic size, Malta, Portugal and Hungary received the highest non-crisis aid in the EU. Aid to industry and services was at EUR 52 billion (82 per cent of non-crisis aid) in comparison to agriculture (13 per cent of total aid) and transport (5 per cent of total aid).

In 2004, new rules for state aid for rescuing and restructuring firms in difficulty were adopted by the EU Commission. They were set to expire in 2012 but were extended till 2013-end, at which time state aid regulations needed to be updated. In May 2012, the Commission also started a Communication on State Aid Modernisation (SAM) reform package which would make state aid more supportive for sustainable growth without distorting competition.

6.4   QUANTIFYING 'OVERALL' BARRIERS TO TRADE IN MANUFACTURING PRODUCTS

As we have just seen, in recent years developed countries including the EU and the US have greatly reduced tariffs on trade in goods and yet this plainly does not mean that these countries have approached complete free trade. In fact the demise of tariffs has made other forms of protection more important, making it more difficult to measure the amount of protection. Accounting for all possible barriers to trade clearly is not straight-forward.

Kee et al. (2009) estimate a trade restrictive index capturing distortions on each country's import bundle (OTRI – Overall Trade Restrictiveness Index) and also the distortions imposed by the rest of the world on each country's export bundle (MA-OTRI – Market Access Overall Trade Restrictiveness Index). More simply, the study measures the impact of each country's trade policy on its own imports (OTRI) and the impact of other countries' trade policies on each country's exports (MA-OTRI). Overall the study finds that non-tariff barriers contribute more than 70 per cent to world protection. For the EU, the trade restrictiveness indices show that the OTRI for tariff and non-tariff barriers is at 8 per cent, higher than Canada and Switzerland, while the MA-OTRI is at 12 per cent. In comparison to this, for the US economy both the OTRI and MA-OTRI are almost equal at 7 per cent. Table 6.3 shows these comparisons for applied tariff barriers.

Table 6.3 Trade restrictiveness indices: manufacturing, 2009 (%)

Country	Indices based on applied tariffs		Indices based on tariffs and non-tariff barriers	
	OTRI	MA-OTRI	OTRI	MA-OTRI
Australia	9.80	4.90	9	10
Canada	3.30	5.00	4	10
Switzerland	0.80	3.20	4	7
China	9.30	8.80	19	7
EU	3.40	7.90	8	12
Japan	4.70	8.00	7	8
Korea, Rep.	4.50	8.30	–	–
Norway	0.80	1.70	1	8
Russian Federation	13.70	3.90	20	10
Singapore	12.70	5.40	–	–
United States	4.50	6.90	7	7

Note: OTRI represents the tariff equivalent applied on imports coming into a country; MA-OTRI represents the tariff equivalent applied to a country's exports by the rest of the world.

Source: World Bank (2009).

Messerlin (2001) estimates overall protection taking into account both tariff and non-tariff barriers (NTBs). The study draws on the existing information to arrive at *ad valorem* estimates of NTBs and adds them to the average tariffs of the sectors in question. For anti-dumping (AD), the share of tariff lines under AD measures has been computed in each sector to get the share-weighted average of the *ad valorem* AD duties, which then has been added to the existing sectoral average tariff.

The results suggest that the estimated level of overall protection is still high. For industrial goods in the EU economy it was roughly 10 to 11 per cent from 1990 to 1995 and continued to be at around 8 per cent in 1999, almost twice as high as the conventional estimate. Further, the most heavily protected sectors such as textiles and apparel and consumer electronics exhibit almost constant rates of protection between 1990 and 1997, and a limited decline from 1997 to 1999. Most of this protection will have remained unchanged at least until 2005, when the dismantling of the quota regime in textiles and clothing began. This reveals that a substantial proportion of industrial products was still highly protected, and implies that 24 per cent of EU industrial products have overall protection of over 10 per cent. Sixteen per cent (one sixth) of EU industrial products have overall protection of over 20 per cent, and among these, the clothing sector has overall protection of more than 30 per cent. The results suggest that the high level of EU overall protection results from the systematic incorporation of NTBs and anti-dumping measures, which are not reported in the official estimates. For the manufacturing sectors affected, anti-dumping procedures and AD duties contribute 13 per cent of their overall rate of protection. Finally, labour-weighted rates of overall protection are higher than corresponding simple averages, suggesting that the EU overall protection is concentrated in labour-intensive sectors, a result consistent with the perception that protecting these sectors by way of AD duties and NTBs is more attractive than trying to modify tariffs.

Price Gaps as a Measure of Protection

With so many barriers to trade it seems that the only way to account for all of them is to exploit the information on prices of similar goods in different countries. Freer trade should lessen and eliminate price disparities in identical traded goods, after allowing for margins from transportation, distribution, marketing, and retail costs. In other words, if there are no barriers to trade then equivalent goods in different countries should not sell at prices that differ by more than the amount it costs to move the goods from one country to the other. If excessive gaps in prices exist for uniform goods, then one can conclude that barriers fragment those markets.

Evidence on international price differences in general and the difference between EU and US prices can be found in three recent surveys: (1) the Arthur Andersen survey for electrical goods; (2) *The Sunday Times* and Nielsen surveys for food products; and (3) *The Economist* survey for a number of goods.

The Arthur Andersen study confirms that electrical goods prices were between 21 and 80 per cent higher in the EU compared with the US in 1998. There are two clear findings (Table 6.4). First, the US is significantly cheaper than the EU, notably for brown goods. Second, the UK is in about the middle of the pack of European countries.

On behalf of the UK government, AC Nielsen (AC Nielsen 2000) undertook a study to compare prices of a large number of goods in the UK, US, France and Germany (see Table 6.5). The comparisons were based on the price spread rather than the average price. The study originally collected 21 023 prices for 106 items in four countries. For their final report, Nielsen was forced to drop 10 374 price observations for lack of comparability and lack of availability of goods. Almost all consumer durables, such as fridges, washing machines, cameras and camcorders, were discarded since they were 'genuinely non-comparable' (AC Nielsen, 2000). Nielsen also

Table 6.4   Percentage deviation from the US price

	PCs	Brown goods	White goods	Small domestic appliances
UK	24.0	66.3	11.2	55.3
Belgium	69.6	102.3	36.4	23.3
Sweden	38.9	118.8	47.3	14.6
France	27.0	74.1	18.9	68.0
Germany	8.2	77.0	32.9	37.9
Italy	38.9	65.8	−0.4	9.7
Spain	−3.2	64.6	0.1	5.8
European average	29.1	81.3	21	30.7

Notes: PCs: notebooks and desktops; Brown goods: audio home systems, cameras, camcorders, TVs and VCRs; White goods: refrigerators, dishwashers and washing machines; Small domestic appliances: irons, toasters, vacuum cleaners.

Source: Arthur Andersen (1999).

excluded a large number of items citing high within-country price variations. For 45 out of their remaining 56 goods Nielsen found an overlap
between the spread of prices in two countries. Hence, it was concluded
that there were no significant differences in prices between countries for
the bulk of the products. Eleven goods showed significant price difference
among countries, eight of which were significantly more expensive in the
UK and three were significantly cheaper in the UK (Table 6.6). The survey
concluded that the results do not provide much support for the 'rip-off
Britain' hypothesis. The results indicate that the difference between the
UK and the rest of the EU is minor compared to the difference between
the EU and the US.

According to another survey conducted by *The Economist*, 54 items are
more expensive in the EU compared to the UK (including most electrical
goods) and 40 items are cheaper in the EU than in the UK. For 16 goods
the EU is 25 per cent or more expensive than the UK.

The information on price disparities within different markets presented
above needs to be converted into an estimate of trade protection if it can
be used to measure welfare costs of trade barriers. Bradford (2000) uses
price data on 120 traded goods (collected by the OECD for six countries:
the US, the UK, Canada, Australia, Japan and the Netherlands) to arrive
at an estimate of price gap (adjusted for transport costs) as a measure of
the extent of protection. The results are aggregated into 28 sectors – agri-
culture/ fishery/ forestry and 27 manufactured products. All of the data
are for the year 1990, except the US, where they are for 1987. These data

Should Britain leave the EU?

Table 6.5 *Food products: comparison of goods across* The Sunday Times *and Nielsen surveys (prices in £)*

	UK	Germany	France	US	% difference from the US		
					UK	Germany	France
Milk							
Sunday Times	0.42	0.65	0.61	0.62	−32.3	4.8	−1.6
Nielsen	0.53	0.39	0.54	0.55	−3.6	−29.1	−1.8
Mayonnaise							
Sunday Times	0.93	0.69	1.28	1.1	−15.5	−37.3	16.4
Nielsen	0.94	0.88	1.08	0.99	−5.1	−11.1	9.1
Kellogg's Corn Flakes							
Sunday Times	1.15	1.48	1.37	2.52	−54.4	−41.3	−45.6
Nielsen	1.09	1.4	1.38	1.63	−33.1	−14.1	−15.3
Sirloin steak							
Sunday Times	11.69	8.62	7.83	6.37	83.5	35.3	22.9
Nielsen	11.08	12.74	9.76	5.51	101.1	131.2	77.1
Coca-Cola							
Sunday Times	0.65	0.55	0.46	0.71	−8.5	−22.5	−35.2
Nielsen	0.46		0.4	0.36	27.8		11.1
Mars Bar							
Sunday Times	1.79	1.0	1.58	1.62	10.5	−38.3	−2.5
Nielsen	0.29	0.28	0.21	0.35	−17.1	−20.0	−40.0
Carrots							
Sunday Times	0.55	0.69	0.51	0.8	−31.3	−13.8	−36.3
Nielsen	0.35	0.48	0.59	1.19	−70.6	−59.7	−50.4
Potatoes							
Sunday Times	0.55	0.42	0.82	0.27	103.7	55.6	203.7
Nielsen	0.5	0.34	0.57	0.98	−49.5	−65.7	−42.4

Notes:
Milk: pasteurized (*Sunday Times*); skimmed (Nielsen)
Mayonnaise: 400–500 g equivalent
Corn Flakes, Kellogg's, 500 g
Sirloin steak, Potatoes and Carrots, per kg
Mars Bar: ST funsize (*Sunday Times*); single equivalent (Nielsen).

Sources: *Sunday Times* survey, August 1998; AC Nielsen survey, November 1999.

Table 6.6   AC Nielsen survey: most and least expensive goods in the UK, 1999 (£)

	UK	Germany	France	US
UK more expensive:				
Top 10 CDs	12.91	8.88	11.06	9.18
Sega Dreamcast	200.12	160.77	163.00	132.26
Coca-Cola (2l)	1.31	0.85	0.82	0.80
Ground coffee	1.95	1.26	1.37	1.31
Non-branded lager	0.92	0.36	0.36	0.49
Dog food (800 g equiv.)	0.79	0.64	0.64	0.62
Shampoo (250 ml equiv.)	2.18	1.35	1.56	1.13
Toilet paper	1.82	1.01	0.81	0.88
UK less expensive:				
Kellogg's Corn Flakes (500 g equiv.)	1.09	1.4	1.38	1.63
Chocolate chip cookies (200 g equiv.)	0.62	0.99	0.72	0.84
Long-sleeved men's shirts	14.87	22.86	21.63	23.02

Source: Nielsen (2000).

are particularly useful because they are comprehensive and every effort has been made to ensure that they are comparable. Input–output tables are used to eliminate distribution margins from final goods prices and thereby provide estimates of ex-factory prices. The results suggest that Australia, Canada and the US are the most open. Their producer prices are 11 to 15 per cent higher than they would be if these six markets were fully integrated. The Netherlands and the UK (two of the member states of the EU), on the other hand, face average protection rates of 47 to 51 per cent respectively. It is this method that we have used, on more recent price data, in estimating the effects of EU protection in Chapter 4.

6.5   COST OF TRADE PROTECTION

There have been a number of attempts to estimate in quantitative terms the potential gains from trade liberalization. However, in recent years there have been only a few studies which concentrate on the manufacturing sector. This is not surprising since the liberalization of trade in industrial goods, especially reduction in tariff protection, is well advanced compared to the reforms of trade in agriculture and services in the developed countries. In this section we review some of the recent studies.

OECD estimates (Love and Lattimore, 2009) indicate that scrapping all tariffs on merchandise trade and reducing trade costs by 1 per cent of the value of trade worldwide would add the equivalent of up to 2 per cent to the present annual gross domestic product (GDP) in some areas.

Taking the fully implemented Uruguay Round as a starting point, the OECD examined eight scenarios designed to reflect different levels of tariff reduction and the uniform reduction in trade costs by 1 per cent of the value of trade. All these scenarios demonstrate the advantages of trade liberalization. The least beneficial scenario involves a 50 per cent cut in tariffs overall and the uniform reduction in trade costs, which nonetheless yields annual global gains of US$ 117 billion.

An approach which reduces high tariffs by a higher proportion, with a maximum after-reform tariff of 5 per cent on any item and the uniform reduction in trade costs, provides an even bigger lift. This so-called 'Swiss formula' yields global gains of US$ 158.5 billion – and all regions gain from the tariff reduction.

Turning to non-tariff barriers, it is estimated that removal of a selection of barriers could generate global gains of up to US$ 90 billion. Another study calculated that lowering trade transaction costs by 1 per cent would lead to global welfare gains of close to US$ 40 billion. This is less in comparison to gains that would accrue if improvements in ports, customs and regulations were brought about. These steps could actually raise total trade by 10 per cent (Love and Lattimore, 2009).

7. Services

Developed economies around the world have become increasingly service oriented, the European Union (EU) being no exception. Services account for more than two-thirds of employment and GDP in the EU. In most other industrial countries services now typically account for around 70 per cent of output.

While the financial crisis of 2008 hit financial and business services badly, the service sector has recovered faster than manufacturing, construction and mining industries. In countries such as Brazil and China, service growth accelerated in 2013. Manufacturing GDP in most EU countries was below the pre-crisis level even in 2013, while services such as information and communication, real estate activities and market services have not suffered as much as other services due to the financial crisis (EC, 2013c). Market services have grown by 1.7 percentage points per annum on average between 2000 and 2012, raising the share of market services in GDP close to 50 per cent, and the share of non-market services[1] has also increased, rising to 23 per cent during the same period.

Services play an important intermediary role that is not fully reflected in the statistics. Well-functioning financial, transportation and distribution systems are critical for the smooth running of the economy. Over time the inter-linkages between manufacturing and services have been on the rise. The service sector share of manufacturing output rose by 2 per cent on average between 2000 and 2009.

The role of services in production, however, is not reflected in its share of world trade. Services account for no more than one-fifth of total cross-border trade, though to this must be added the substantial volume of trade done through the other modes of supply – in particular through commercial establishments in the export market.

The lower tradability of a significant number of services has mainly happened for two reasons. First, technical constraints arise out of the impossibility of disconnecting production from consumption and supplying customers at a distance. In recent years, however, technological advances are enabling consumers to participate in a growing number of service-related activities without having to be physically present. Second, the low volume of trade in services has been policy induced; there have traditionally been significant barriers to service trade in many countries.

In the case of the EU, core services such as telecommunications, air transport and to a lesser extent financial services have long been shielded from both internal and external competition. In recent years, the single market programme in services, initiated in 1985, and its successive extensions during the 1990s such as the Single Market Action Plan (SMP) in 1997 have sought to liberalize the intra-EU services trade. Liberalization of services is also taking place outside the EU with the evolution of the General Agreement on Trade in Services (GATS). In spite of these measures, the expansion of services activities across national borders in Europe continues to be hampered by a wide range of barriers.

The first section of this chapter considers the structural shift from the manufacturing to the services economy in developed countries. It discusses the significance of services for output and employment in the EU and other industrial nations. The second section reviews the statistics on all modes of services trade. It particularly focuses on the vital role of foreign direct investment in international trade in services. The third and fourth sections review and evaluate the barriers to trade in services. The final section outlines the main empirical findings concerning the welfare effects of services liberalization. It considers the implications of further liberalization and how it might impact on the EU economy.

7.1 THE ROLE OF THE SERVICE SECTOR

We can see the increased importance of the services sector for production and employment in Table 7.1. In all OECD countries, the services sector accounts for more than 70 per cent of output employment. In the last decade, countries such as Luxembourg, the UK, Belgium and France have witnessed a significant shift towards the service sector, with services contributing over 75 per cent of GDP. The 2008 financial crisis has hit all sectors of the economy, but the impact on the service sector has been less than on construction and manufacturing.

Services are less capital intensive than manufacturing and benefit more from the increased demand that comes with higher incomes; they are also a large source of job creation. Many traditional services such as distribution, construction, education, health and social services are particularly labour intensive. At the same time, knowledge-intensive services are increasingly important for overall job creation, both because they are growing rapidly and because they play a role in the upgrading of workers' skills. At present, regulatory barriers, tax wedges, minimum wages and so on, impede the

Table 7.1   *Share of services in total value added at current prices and*
employment (%)

Country	Share of total value added			Share of total employment		
	1999	2004	2012	1999	2004	2012
Austria	64.9	68	69.8	59.2	67.3	68.9
Belgium	70.8	74	77.4	–	73.1	77.1
Denmark	71.9	72	76.7	73.0	73.1	78
Finland	63.3	64	71.2	65.6	69.3	73
France	72.0		79.2	70.6	77.0	79.7*
Germany	67.7	70	68.6	–	66.0	70.6
Greece	68.5	76		57.6	64.9	70.4
Ireland	60.3	66	70.5	63.2	67.2	77.1
Italy	67.3	72	73.7	–	64.5	68.1
Luxembourg	78.4	83	86.8	73.6	74.5	78.2
The Netherlands	70.4	74	74.0	72.9	77.7	82.1
Portugal	65.4	73	73.8	–	56.5	63.6
Spain	65.7	67	70.5	62.6	64.3	75.0
Sweden	68.8	69	71.6	73.1	75.2	78.4
UK	70.3	76	77.8	75.3	76.7	79.7
US	75.4	77	78.0	76.3	78.4	81.2
Canada	64.7	–	–	74.1	–	–
Mexico	66.3	–	–	53.9	–	–

Note: * 2011.

Source: OECD National Accounts Statistics database 2014, Eurostat, World Bank.

development of these types of services in a number of countries, particularly in continental European countries.

Seven years after the financial crisis hit the world, the labour market
in OECD countries is still recovering. However, job creation in services
has exceeded overall job growth in the OECD area. The employment rate
in OECD countries is 2 per cent below its level before the financial crisis.
With global economic recovery, more recently, the labour market has witnessed some improvement but is still a long way from covering ground lost
during the crisis.

By 2012, the US had 81 per cent of civilian workers (which includes
government workers, but excludes armed forces personnel) engaged in
activities related to services, and in the UK the share of services in total
employment was at 80 per cent. The share is expected to continue to rise
over time as fast-growing knowledge-based services expand. According to

the European Commission, 19.4 million jobs are expected to be created requiring highly skilled qualifications between 2013 and 2025 in the EU. As of 2012, service employment accounted for over two-thirds of the total employment in the EU-28. The share of employment by sector shows that transportation employs 5 per cent and finance and insurance 2.7 per cent of the total workforce.

7.2   TRADE IN SERVICES

The intangibility of services makes them and trade in them difficult to define. Although some services may be defined through their physical presence, for example transport or hotel services, others are conceptually more abstract, such as consultancy or education. The need in many services for proximity between the consumer and the producer implies that one of them must move to make an international transaction possible.

Since the conventional definition of trade – where a product crosses the frontier and is registered at the border – would miss out on such transactions in services, it is now customary to define trade in services following the GATS to include four different modes of supply:

> Mode 1: Cross-border supply from the territory of one member into that of another.
> Mode 2: Consumption abroad, in which the service is supplied in the territory of one member to the consumer of another.
> Mode 3: Supply though commercial presence in which the service supplier is legally established in the export market.
> Mode 4: Supply through the movement of natural persons, meaning the temporary presence of individuals without legal personality to supply services in a member's market.

Measurement of trade in services is inherently more difficult than measurement of trade in goods and as a result statistics on international trade in services are incomplete.

No country has ever published a data set to pull together a comprehensive picture of services trade through all four modes and across all sectors. However, it is known that cross-border supply (mode 1) and commercial presence (mode 3) are the economically most important modes. Almost the only source of data to capture a part of service trade is through the balance of payments statistics. It records cross-border trade, consumption abroad and to some extent trade though movement of natural persons (even then the balance of payments (BOP) based data cannot be clearly broken down into modes 1, 2 and 4, and nor do they provide a complete picture of mode 4). However, it does not capture any services trade under mode 3, the trade of services though commercial presence. This is because a subsidiary that establishes commercial presence is a resident of the country in which it is set up; accordingly its sales to the local population are transactions between residents and so escape BOP recording. At the same time, such sales are considered trade in services under the GATS definition.[2] The only data that are readily available on mode 3 trade are those published by the US Department of Commerce on sales of foreign affiliates in the US and the sales of US affiliates abroad. It is known that a large amount of trade in services takes place through an established presence, for example through foreign direct investment (FDI), and the available evidence suggests that commercial presence has been the most dynamic model of service supply in recent years.

FDI is an important aspect of international trade in services. For many service industries, a subsidiary abroad is indispensable if a market is to be developed. Banks, insurance companies and retailers rely on direct contact with their customers. Important contributions to services FDI are being made in retailing, banking, business services and telecommunications, and, to a limited extent, in hotels and restaurants. These are all sectors where commercial presence is an important requirement for business activity.

The EU is a net investor in the service sectors of the rest of the world. The financial crisis has led to some decline in the inflows and outflows in 2008 and 2009 in the EU and also across the world. However, there has been some pick up since then. As of 2011, the main partners for EU investors have been the US, Brazil, Canada and Switzerland. The outflows to Brazil increased threefold between 2008 and 2011 (WTO, 2013). The US accounted for 40 per cent of the EU's inward stocks of FDI from the rest of the world in 2010. A major part of these investments were made in manufacturing and financial and insurance activities. Overall EU FDI in services stands at inward stocks at US$ 1.5 trillion as of 2012 while outward stocks are at US$ 3.5 trillion. In the transportation sector, inward stocks were at US$ 44 billion in 2012 while outward FDI was at US$ 32 billion. In telecommunications, inward FDI was at US$ 91 billion and outward stocks were at US$ 79 billion in 2012. Unlike the transport and telecommunication sectors, inward stocks of FDI (US$ 563 billion) were lower than outward (US$ 895 billion) in the financial and insurance sector in 2012.

Another measure of service trade is found by looking at value added by each country in the production of goods and services – a joint initiative by the OECD and WTO. The share of services in gross exports in OECD countries stands close to 22 per cent but when we consider this share in

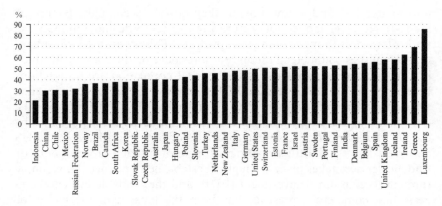

Source: OECD database.

Figure 7.1   Share of service value added in total exports, 2009

terms of value added it rises to almost 50 per cent of exports. Countries such as Luxembourg, Greece, Ireland and UK have an above 50 per cent share of service exports to total exports in terms of value added as of 2009 (OECD–WTO, 2013) (see Figure 7.1). The difference in the share of services in gross output and in value added arises partly because of the increasing contribution of services to the manufacturing sector. Efficient and proper functioning transport, logistics, telecommunication and professional services improve productivity and are essential for the manufacturing sector. Therefore growth and development of the service sector is imperative.

World Trade in Services

The share of services in world trade is close to 20 per cent and has remained near that level since the 1990s. However, in terms of domestic value added, services account for 70 per cent of world GDP, rising from 10 per cent in the 1990s. This difference in the importance of services in trade and GDP arises because many services are traded indirectly as a part of goods.

OECD countries accounted for approximately 80 per cent of world service exports (excluding mode 3) and intra-OECD exports accounted for some 80 per cent of total OECD exports (ranging from 61 per cent of Australia's exports to over 90 per cent for a number of reporting OECD countries). The EU is the largest region of destination for OECD exports (34 per cent of world service exports) followed by NAFTA (17 per cent of world service exports). Intra-EU trade largely accounts for this dominant

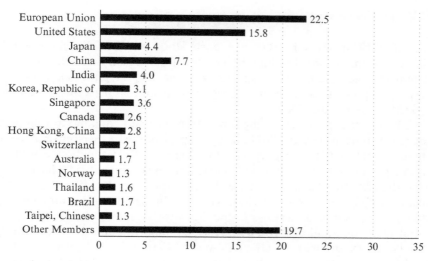

Source: WTO (2013).

Figure 7.2   Share of commercial services trade as a percentage of total world service trade, 2013

position of the EU in the OECD compared to other OECD regions. The OECD Asia and Oceania countries mainly trade with Asian (over 3 per cent of world exports) and American (3 per cent of world exports) countries. Africa's main region of destination for service exports is Europe (over half of service exports, mainly to the EU). Three per cent of total world service exports go to Africa. In the US, commercial services exports in 2013 were US\$ 662 billion – more than double their level 10 years ago.

The EU is the world's largest exporter of commercial services (Figure 7.2). In the EU, the surplus in services trade stood at EUR 121 billion in 2011 and has multiplied by more than 20 over the past 10 years. In services trade, 'other business services' were the largest category with a share of 30 per cent, followed by transportation (22 per cent), travel (14 per cent), and financial services (8 per cent). In terms of partner, the US is the largest partner of the EU in both service exports (24 per cent) and imports (29 per cent), though its share has been declining since 2000. Switzerland is the second largest exporter (13 per cent) and importer (11 per cent) of the EU as of 2011.

UK Trade in Services

As of 2012, in the UK, service exports stood at US$ 298 billion and imports were at US$ 187 billion. The financial industry was the largest exporting sector and travel services was the biggest importer. Service exports represent 38 per cent of gross exports and 60 per cent of value-added exports in the UK.

UK service exports (excluding travel, transport and banking) to Europe declined between 2009 and 2011 during the peak of the financial crisis. After that, in 2011 and 2012, exports rose by 7 per cent. By destination, exports in the EU were the highest to Ireland (12 per cent), Switzerland, Germany and the Netherlands, while outside the EU exports to the US stood at 28 per cent, followed by Asia at 16 per cent. On the import side, Europe was the major exporter of services to the UK with a share of 52 per cent of total ITIS (International Trade in Services) imports value. Germany was the largest exporter to the UK, followed by France, Ireland, Netherlands and Italy in the EU. Outside the EU, the US was the second largest supplier.

In 2012, professional, scientific and technical activities were the largest contributors of service exports at £32 billion. This was followed by information and communication, financial and insurance activities and then wholesale and retail trade.

7.3   BARRIERS TO SERVICE TRADE

Throughout the post-war period, trade in services was largely unaffected by the process of liberalization taking place in merchandise trade. Even in industrialized countries with relatively liberal merchandise trade regimes, barriers to trade in services and movements of natural persons can be particularly restrictive. Historically, services have been highly regulated, partly due to a possibility of market failures in some industries, but also as a result of the domestic influence of special interest groups sheltered from foreign competitive pressures. Traditionally many important service markets such as transport and basic telecommunications have been reserved for the monopoly supplier or made subject to strict regulations and border control. Unlike trade in goods, governments usually apply restrictions on the sale of services of foreign origin inside their territories rather than at their borders. Achieving a common market in services, therefore, has presented a more complex challenge than in goods.

Because of the nature of trade in services, trade restrictive measures in services differ in important ways from measures in goods. First, border taxes equivalent to tariffs are difficult to impose on services imports

Source: ONS.

Figure 7.3 UK service exports (excluding travel, transport and banking) (£ million), 2012

because they are often not delivered across borders. Quotas and other quantitative restrictions, on the other hand, are pervasive. Second, services trade can be greatly affected by numerous internal policies that discriminate against foreign producers. These include measures that directly provide a cost advantage to domestic producers, such as subsidies, and other measures that impose a cost or create a competitive disadvantage for foreign producers (for example, internal direct or indirect tax instruments). Third, because of the simultaneous nature of production and consumption of many services, restrictive measures that affect the movement of factors (labour or capital, FDI) must also be considered as some of the impediments to trade in services.

What are the most important barriers to trade in services? The most effective service trade barriers are those which wholly or partially block market access for foreign suppliers. There are two general issues of classification to bear in mind. First, trade restrictive measures can be categorized as either reducing market access to foreign service providers or as national discrimination against foreign providers once they have entered the domestic market.

Hoekman and Braga (1997) identify the following types of barriers: (1) quotas, local content, and prohibitions; (2) price-based instruments; (3) standards, licensing, and procurement; and (4) discriminatory access to distribution networks.

Quantitative restriction (QR) type policies are commonly applied to service providers and affect all four modes of services trade. On cross-border trade, they are most evident in the transport sectors. Foreign providers are either completely shut out (that is, a zero quota) of certain segments, such as cabotage, or only provided limited access, as in international transport. In many countries, there are outright prohibitions directed against foreign providers of services such as domestic transportation, basic telecommunications, and legal, insurance, education, surveying, and investment advisory services. On consumption abroad, quotas are sometimes implemented through foreign exchange restrictions, for example the ability of citizens to consume services, such as tourism and education, abroad is curtailed by limits on foreign exchange entitlements. On commercial presence, quotas are imposed on the number of foreign suppliers who are allowed to establish in sectors like telecommunications and banking. Quotas on foreign participation also take the form of restrictions on foreign equity ownership in individual enterprises. Finally, quotas are perhaps most stringent in the case of movement of service-providing personnel, and affect trade not only in professional services, but also in a variety of services that are intensive in the use of unskilled or semi-skilled labour, such as construction.

Price-based barriers may take the form of visa fees and entry or exit taxes, discriminatory airline landing fees, and port taxes. Tariffs can be significant barriers to trade in goods that embody services (for example, films, television programmes, computer software) or goods that are used in producing services (for example, computers, telecommunications equipment, advertising material). Further, many service sectors are subject to government-sanctioned or monitored price controls; examples include air transportation, financial services, and telecommunications. Government subsidies are commonly used in service sectors such as construction, communications, and road and rail transport.

Licensing or certification requirements may be imposed on foreign providers of professional and business services. In the absence of recognition measures, such requirements can discourage or prohibit foreign participation in the provision of services. Environmental standards may also affect service providers, particularly in transportation and tourism. Government procurement policies are often designed to favour domestic over foreign providers of services as well as goods by means of preference margins and outright prohibitions. Also, in many countries foreign providers have discriminatory or limited access to distribution channels and communications systems.

Quantitative measures of service trade barriers use other information, in addition to information in the schedule of commitments by countries, to obtain an index of the restrictiveness of services trade for various subsectors or countries. These measures confirm the findings of the descriptive statistics: transportation, storage, and communication services are estimated to have the highest trade barriers, and construction services the lowest.

The EU Services Barriers and Progress in Deregulation

The service directive was introduced in the EU to remove legal and administrative barriers in 2006 and was implemented in 2009. It aims to establish a single service market in the EU and reduce sectoral barriers. This directive focuses on administrative simplification, freedom of establishment and freedom to provide services. Across the region, for businesses to be able to thrive, they require reliable and complete information on regulatory requirements which is now being provided through Points of Single Contact (PSC) and e-government services. The implementation of the directive has led to some lowering of restrictions across sectors, mostly so far in tourism activities, hotels and restaurants, construction and real estate.

The financial crisis has instigated a wave of reforms in the service sector. To make the single market programme work better, the Single Market Acts

I and II laid down legislative proposals to boost growth and employment. In addition, proposals have been published to complete the digital single market initiative.

However, so far the integration of services into a single market has been slower than that seen in the goods market. The 'trade integration' measure (the average of imports and exports divided by GDP) in the goods market is 22 per cent while in services it is only 5 per cent. The European Commission estimates that efficient implementation of the service directive could yield addition to GDP by 0.6 to 2.6 per cent over the coming years.

The provision to allow countries to maintain pre-existing restrictions if judged necessary to protect the public interest has hindered the implementation of the directive across the region (IMF, 2014). The directive has been criticized per se as it does not require countries to abolish restrictions to competition. The thrust has been to negotiate common regulative standards for services. The focus has thus been placed on regulatory convergence between the member states and not on competition.

In addition, the sectoral approach to liberalization implies that many services such as medical services have been as yet left untouched. The service directive currently covers 65 per cent of service activities in the region. Even within the sectors where the single market programme has been implemented, many restrictive measures have survived and state aid or subsidies to service firms continue to be substantial.

Hence a single market in services also requires competition. The directive should therefore bring in competition authorities to assess the merits of existing regulations (IMF, 2014).

Financial Services

For reform in the financial sector the EU has introduced the 'Single Rulebook' framework and has tabled more than 40 directives to restore market confidence and financial stability. The EU has reacted to the recent financial crisis with regulative responses similar to elsewhere in the G20, including demands that banks hold more capital and reduce their risk exposure. The EU has introduced rules so that shareholders and creditors – and not taxpayers – bear the brunt of a bank failure. It has also begun the creation of a banking union. Unfortunately the main result so far has been a serious credit shortage, while the EU banking system remains weak and vulnerable.

The EU has put together three new institutions, namely, the European Banking Authority (EBA), European Securities and Markets Authority (ESMA) and the European Insurance and Occupational Pension Authority for banks, markets and insurance and pensions (EIOPA). The idea is to create a 'level playing field' for all member states and make financial markets work better. The European Commission expects these reforms to boost growth by 0.6 to 1.1 per cent of EU GDP per year; however, it is far from clear whether they will reduce barriers and enhance competition in these service industries, rather than simply raise costs for the more competitive players.

In consumer banking, EU legislation has ensured that bank deposits are guaranteed up to EUR 100 000 per deposit in the bank. In addition, they have made it easier to transfer bank accounts from one EU country to another.

In April 2014, the EU adopted the proposal of regulating the financial markets. This will help in protecting investors and increases the supervisory power of regulators to prohibit marketing and distribution of certain high risk products. In addition, under a harmonized regime, non-EU firms are granted access to EU professional markets (EC, 2014b). Again it is unclear as to why this regime will not end up preventing or reducing existing trade in newly-regulated products.

Professional services
In the area of professional services, there are significant variations in EU Member State requirements for foreign lawyers and accountants intending to practise in the EU. While many of these are not explicit barriers, disparities among EU Member State requirements complicate access to the European market for foreign lawyers and accountants. Overall in professional services, there are varying restrictions on the number of entrants into the profession, rates charged and billing arrangements, organizational structure of businesses providing professional services, exclusive rights enjoyed by practitioners and the ability to advertise (Eurostat, 2014).

Legal services, and accounting and auditing services
Barriers include, among other things, nationality requirements, bans on majority holdings, a requirement to pass local professional examinations and companies having to have a registered office in one of the EU Member States. According to the OECD (2014a) Services Trade Restrictiveness Index (STRI), many countries in the EU have a restrictiveness index above the average (of 40 countries considered). Austria, Belgium, Spain and Estonia have high restrictiveness in the sector, primarily due to restrictions on movement of people and restrictions on foreign entry.

Energy services
During the 1990s when the national electricity and natural gas markets were still monopolized, the EU started to open up markets to competition.

The first liberalization process was adopted in 1996 (electricity) and 1998 (gas); the second came about in 2003. The Barcelona European Council in spring 2002 agreed that all non-household consumers should have freedom of choice of gas and electricity supplier by 2004 (that is, 60 per cent of the market is to be opened up). Energy ministers recently reached a political agreement that will lead to full market opening, that is for household users as well. This third liberalization package is designed to strengthen competition in electricity and gas markets. Nevertheless these markets remain highly fragmented.

Postal services

In 2013, all member states abolished sections of the national post monopolies. Any private entity that obtains a licence from the market regulator can now provide postal services in the region. All national post companies have been changed into public listed companies and some governments have sold shares to private investors. One such case of the latter is the Royal Mail in the UK.

However, on the ground, the pace of competitive entry in the sector continues to be slow and national postal services continue to dominate the market. Market competition is present only in certain segments such as parcel and express mail delivery.

The prevalence of postal monopolies in many EU countries has long restricted market access and subjected their competitors to unequal conditions of competition. In October 2001, EU Member States agreed to open additional postal services to competition, beginning in 2003, including all outgoing cross-border mail.

Air transport

Some of the most striking changes in the EU services sector have occurred in air transport. In the past, the industry was tightly regulated on the basis of bilateral agreements between Member States. In 2010, the aviation sector contributed EUR 140 billion to European GDP. The creation of a large Single Market in the 1990s has been in part responsible for driving the sector. Three successive packages of liberalizing measures – adopted during the 1990s – have resulted in equal rights of access to all the Community's markets for all European-owned airlines. The result is that any EU airline can now operate on any route within the Community, and there are no restrictions on the number of flights or the setting of fares in the region.

These reforms have led to more competition. The intra-EU-15 flights have seen a huge increase, rising from 864 in 1992 to 3151 in 2012. The number of summer routes has seen an increase of 240 per cent, while winter routes have risen by 115 per cent during the same period (EC,

2013d). Also, there is increased competition from non-EU airlines, and low-cost carriers are forcing competition on established airlines. In 2012, these low-cost carriers reached a 45 per cent market share of available seat capacity.

Telecommunications
Since the late 1980s, there has been a general trend toward increased competition and openness in European telecommunications. Both the WTO Basic Telecommunications Agreement and EU legislation in 2001 have spurred deregulation. The EU set up the Telecom Package in 2009 to update the framework set up in 2002 and to create a common set of regulations for the whole industry. This framework includes independence of the national regulatory authorities (NRAs).

However, liberalization and harmonization have been uneven across the EU. Excessive or inconsistent regulation continues to hinder investments in the sector. In addition, inefficiency in the allocation of mobile spectrums and barriers to consolidation in the industry have dampened growth in the sector.

Regarding mobile networks, roaming regulations have lowered the maximum roaming charges allowed since 2007. In addition, in 2014, a regulation to abolish end-user roaming charges was passed in the European Parliament. This, which is an example of intrusive regulation, will now have to be approved by the council of the European Union.

According to the OECD (2014a) STRI, restrictiveness in telecoms in a majority of EU countries is below average (across the 40 countries considered). Greece stands out, with an above average index.

7.4 QUANTIFYING THE BARRIERS TO TRADE IN SERVICES

Measuring the barriers to services trade is a complicated task. Trade restrictiveness has been measured mostly through qualitative methods involving business surveys and direct evaluation of regulations, price-based calculations, and the gravity equation based approach.

Studies using qualitative methods include Hoekman (1995), the Australian Productivity Commission, Mattoo et al. (2006). These studies were prior, however, to the recent EU liberalization of services. Borchert et al. (2012) (Figure 7.4) estimate the restrictiveness of service trade policies by sector across 103 countries. This study details the service trade restrictiveness database of the World Bank. They find substantial variation across sectors, with transport and communication facing significant

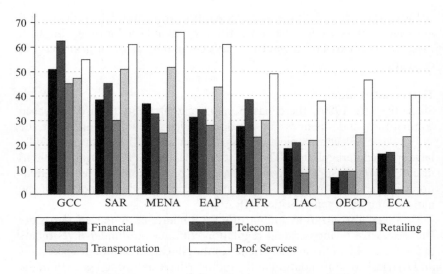

Note:　The services trade restriction index (STRI) at the regional level is calculated as a simple average of individual country's STRIs. The STRI in the cross-border air passenger transportation subsector comes from the QUASAR database of WTO (2007). Regional abbreviations: HNO – High income non-OECD, SAR – South Asia, EAP – East Asia and pacific, MENA – Middle East and North Africa, AFR – Sub-Saharan Africa, LAC – Latin America and Caribbean, ECA – Europe and Central Asia, OECD – High income OECD.

Source:　Borchert et al. (2012).

Figure 7.4　Services Trade Restrictiveness Index by sector

barriers to trade across most countries. On the other hand, financial services and retail distribution are much less restrictive to foreign competition in high income countries. According to the index, EU-20 countries have an overall restrictiveness index of 26.1, as compared to 23.4 in Japan, 14.3 in the UK and 17.7 in the US. According to the EU sectoral breakdown, transportation had the highest restriction in professional services (54), followed by transportation (37.1) and retail (24), while the financial and telecommunications sector had low restrictiveness. In the UK, a similar situation prevails, with higher restrictions in transport (23.1) and professional services (45). On the other hand, in the US, financial services have higher restrictions (21.4) in comparison to the transport sector (7.9).

More recently, the OECD has formulated a Services Trade Restrictiveness Index (STRI) which includes two elements: a regulatory database and composite indices (largely from business surveys). The former is based on laws and regulations in 40 countries across 18 different sectors. The composite indices identify restrictions in five categories with values between zero and

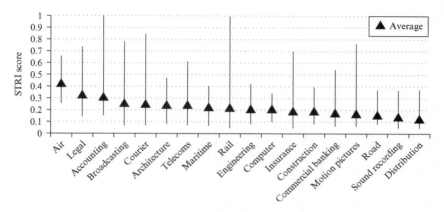

Note: Air transport and road freight refer to only commercial establishments.

Source: OECD (2014a).

Figure 7.5   STRI average, minimum and maximum across sectors

one. While zero implies complete openness to trade and investment, even a score above 0.1 means restrictiveness is significant, and scores between 0.2 and 0.3 indicate significant restrictiveness.

To begin with, the trade restrictiveness across sectors shows a large dispersion across countries and thus there is clear scope for removing these restrictions to increase gains from trade. Out of the 18 sectors, the most restrictive sectors come out as air transport, legal services and accounting services, with scores close to or above 0.3 on the STRI (see Figure 7.5).

In service restrictiveness the UK fares well on the STRI index across the major 18 sectors in the OECD study, coming in below the OECD average. It is one of the most transparent in the rule-making process and in administrative requirements for obtaining licences and registering companies. It is found to be most open in three sectors: computer services, architecture and engineering. It is found to be more restrictive in air transport, accounting and legal services.

At the other extreme, Greece is highly restrictive with an above average STRI score in 11 out of 18 sectors. Given that services accounts for two-thirds of Greek GDP and 55 per cent of gross exports, reforms in increasing competition in the service sector would increase efficiency.

In one of the earlier studies OECD (2001a) classifies the OECD countries into four clusters based on their state of barriers to trade in services. The first cluster, a very liberal one, includes the US and UK as well as Australia and Sweden. A mostly liberal cluster includes Germany, the

Table 7.2   Restrictiveness index scores (scale 0–1 from least to most restrictive)

	Index	UK	RoEU	NAFTA	ROW
Accountancy services	Domestic	0.18	0.20	0.19	0.17
	Foreign	0.19	0.36	0.37	0.43
Architectural services	D	0.00	0.09	0.14	0.04
	F	0.07	0.21	0.29	0.20
Engineering services	D	0.03	0.09	0.09	0.04
	F	0.07	0.16	0.23	0.17
Legal services	D	0.18	0.19	0.25	0.16
	F	0.31	0.40	0.50	0.47
Maritime services	D	0.06	0.14	0.14	0.16
	F	0.24	0.33	0.47	0.47
Telecommunications	D	0.00	0.12	0.13	0.25
	F	0.00	0.19	0.34	0.41
Banking services	D	0.00	0.00	0.00	0.08
	F	0.07	0.07	0.10	0.33
Distribution services	D	0.05	0.09	0.02	0.08
	F	0.19	0.24	0.15	0.21

Source: Nguyen-Hong (2000); McGuire and Schuele (2000).

Netherlands, Finland, Ireland and Norway. The third cluster is a mix of liberal and restrictive approaches, which includes Belgium and Denmark. Lastly, a cluster of mostly restrictive regimes includes those of Italy and Greece.

The fact that Britain's services sector is more open than the rest of the EU is also confirmed by Nguyen-Hong (2000) and McGuire and Schuele (2000) (Table 7.2). Both these studies calculate an index by identifying existing policies affecting entry and operations post-entry, assigning each a weight based on interviews in the private sector, and summing across weights to obtain an overall index. The domestic index measures the restrictions affecting domestic service providers and the foreign index quantifies the restrictions facing foreign service providers in seeking to provide services in the local market. The domestic and foreign restrictiveness index scores range from 0 to 1. According to these surveys the services sector in Britain is less restrictive in all services under review compared to the average for the rest of the EU Member States (Table 7.2). Given the fact that Britain is the world's biggest services exporter after the US, it has a clear economic interest in seeing services markets liberalized around the world. Colecchia (2001) calculates indices for trade barriers in accountancy services for four countries: the UK, France, Australia and the US. The restrictiveness index values in these four countries are 0.5, 0.7, 1.15 and 1.55 respectively. These numbers suggest that among the four countries, the UK is the most open, while the US is the most restrictive for accountancy services.

The Australian Productivity Commission in many studies suggests that barriers to services trade are substantial, specifically in discrimination against foreign providers (Findlay and Warren, 2000). Table 7.3 highlights sector-specific price and cost estimates of the impact of restrictiveness indices.

Looking at tariff equivalents in the service sector, Guillin (2011) finds that the overall tariff equivalent in the service sector is close to 40 per cent, while Walsh (2006) estimates it at 72 per cent using data for 78 countries across four service sectors. The vast difference in estimation arises due to the use of different samples and techniques applied. However, most studies agree that the restrictions in the service sector are higher in developing countries than OECD countries (Walsh, 2006; François et al., 2003).

The restrictiveness in services varies across sectors. In a recent study by Fontagné et al. (2011), the tariff equivalent of services is calculated by comparing actual trade in services against a benchmark. This study uses the gravity model approach by using information on barriers faced by exporters of services to explain price cost margin differences in services. The study estimates the average protection applied by each importer through the importer fixed effects coefficients in a gravity equation for 9 services across 65 countries. It finds that the most liberalized sector is transport, with a 26 per cent tariff equivalent and the most protected is construction, with a 75 per cent tariff equivalent. In another study (Fontagné et al., 2009), they estimate that the level of protection is heterogeneous among European countries. The EU-25 has much higher tariffs than Asia and the US, in most sectors, as of 2005 (Table 7.4).

In finance, the tariff equivalent is at 104 per cent in the EU-25 as compared to 44.7 per cent in the US and 54 per cent in Japan. In the construction sector, the tariff equivalent in the EU is almost three times that in the US. The US has a higher tariff equivalent than the EU-25 in royalties.

Turning to price-based measures that derive estimates of barriers to trade, the percentage difference between domestic and foreign prices is comparable to a tariff provided price differences are due to government-imposed barriers. Price gaps can also be quantified using econometric methods or derived from quantity-based measures with the help of elasticities of demand and supply. Some studies have tried to calculate tariff-equivalents for services sector using price and quantity data. Some of these studies present estimates for the EU; François (1999) for various services;

Table 7.3 Estimates of price/cost impact of service policies

Sector	Source and period covered	Measure	OECD countries			Developing countries		
			Simple average	σ	N	Simple average	σ	N
Maritime shipping	Clark, Dollar and Micco (2004); 2000	Percentage impact on shipping costs of mandatory use of certain port services	2.0	2.6	21	5.6	3.5	32
Air transport: economy fare	Doove et al. (2001); late 1990s	Estimated increase (%) in fares over an estimated 'free trade' level for a set of bilateral routes	30.6	19.5	23	63.9	19.6	12
Air transport: APEX discount fare	Doove et al. (2001); late 1990s	Estimated increase (%) in fares over an estimated 'free trade' level for a set of bilateral routes	8.9	4.4	23	16.8	3.5	12
Retail food distribution	Kalirajan (2000);	Impact on costs of barriers on foreign establishment	2.7	1.7	12	2.3	3.2	6
Retail banking	Kalirajan et al. (2001); 1996–97	Percentage impact on net interest margins of discriminatory policies	11.8	11.6	7 (a)	31.8	19.0	9
Engineering	Nguyen-Hong (2000); 1996	Impact of barriers to FDI on price cost margin (%)	5.2	4.1	14	8.4	4.3	6
Mobile telecom	Doove et al. (2001); late 1997	Price impact (%) of regulatory policies relative to a notional benchmark regime	26	27	24	21	15	18
International telecom	Doove et al. (2001); late 1997	Price impact (%) of regulatory policies relative to a notional benchmark regime	73	61	24	34	9	18

Note: Includes the EU-15 as one observation.

Source: Data compiled in part from tables reported in Stern and Deardorff (2006) and Dee (2005). The Doove et al. (2001) study draws extensively on the results of Boylaud and Nicoletti (2001) and Gönenç and Nicoletti (2000).

Table 7.4 Tariff equivalents (%)

	Transport	Communication	Travel	Insurance	Finance	Construction	Government	Royalties	Recreational services
EUR-15	31.55	19.24	34.85	47.83	97.61	60.34	61.12	101.05	64.03
EUR-25	32.34	21.38	32.97	43.23	104.40	70.31	60.51	93.28	68.05
USA	24.89	3.36	43.96	24.12	44.70	23.86	8.98	147.58	45.11
Japan	20.26	13.95	19.38	36.66	54.65	4.13	40.41	118.63	29.98
OECD	32.70	25.34	32.78	42.47	99.91	56.57	62.57	101.40	70.37
non-OECD	20.43	21.97	30.28	33.01	122.48	41.59	47.99	79.24	100.59
Asia	18.16	15.70	26.04	27.54	107.46	22.04	43.59	62.88	102.38
South America	15.24	15.88	27.90	30.51	144.43	36.49	63.52	87.14	111.39
Total	25.88	23.53	31.39	37.57	111.77	48.81	54.91	89.93	85.20

Source: Fontagné et al. (2011).

161

Warren (2000) for telecommunications; Messerlin (2001) for passenger air transport, films, and telecom; and Kalirajan et al. (2001), Warren and Findlay (2000), and Kaleeswaran et al. (2000) for banking services, Nguyen-Hong (2000) for engineering services.

Messerlin (2001) estimates tariff-equivalents for telecommunications, passenger air transport and film for EU services at 45 per cent, 71 per cent and 77 per cent respectively. In telecommunications the costs of protection are estimated on the basis of the wedge between average British–Finnish–Swedish prices and EC prices. The former group is taken to consist of a competitive benchmark market. For passenger air transport the differential between the intra domestic Member State fully flexible fare and the intra- or extra-EC corresponding fares is taken as a measure of protection. This differential is estimated relative to Britain (the least distorted market). For films, an estimate of tariff equivalent is calculated by summing up the seat tax[3] (11 per cent) and the tariff equivalent of subsidies (66 per cent).

The above overview of current work on measuring barriers to trade in services suggests that the quality of estimates of barriers has been improving in recent years, both in terms of the range of the barriers included and of the measurement techniques employed. However, it is difficult to determine if these estimates are realistic as a number of limitations remain related to data availability and the weight-assignment for different restrictions. The wide range of the estimated service trade barriers is reflected in the differing welfare effects from services liberalization.

7.5   GAINS FROM LIBERALIZATION

Measuring the economy-wide impact of trade liberalization requires a global general equilibrium framework, which captures inter-sectoral effects for an economy and links between economies. Numerous such models analysing the economic impacts of policies affecting trade in goods are available, but relatively little work has been completed on assessing the potential gains from alternative liberalization scenarios in services. The difficulties arise from poor data on international service transactions and the lack of a comprehensive measure of restrictions on trade in services. Modelling of trade in services also requires a modelling structure that can incorporate the various models through which services are supplied and account for the movement of factors of production (OECD, 2000). The studies reviewed here are only indicative of potential gains of services trade because the modelling of services liberalization is still very much in its infancy. The review shows that liberalization of services trade generates welfare gains under all modelling assumptions and economies, with high initial levels of protection gain most in terms of percentage gains as a share of GDP.

An IMF study (Fernández Corugedo and Pérez Ruiz, 2014) using input–output analysis estimates the impact of liberalization of service policies incorporating its multiplier effects in the economy. The paper focuses on the French economy and examines the gains to output and employment from a reform of the service sector. The paper draws on similar analysis done by Hulten (1978), Jones (2011) and Gabaix (2011) which take into account the linkages between sectors and incorporate spillover effects onto GDP from enhancing productivity through reforms in one sector. For example, improvement in the transportation sector will result in pushing up growth in related sectors that use it as an input, such as wholesale and distribution, manufacturing and so on. In the case of France, it is found that the largest gains can be accrued through reforms in business activities, other market services, and transport and storage sectors. A 1 per cent increase in the total factor productivity of business activities raises overall GDP by 0.37 per cent.

Another recent study by the OECD in its Services Trade Restrictiveness report (2014a), estimates the impact of reducing restrictiveness on the country's trade. Taking a country with STRI scores that are near average for the four sectors concerned, it assumes that the country undertakes reforms bringing down the STRI indexes by 5 basis points. The estimated impact in the four sectors will be positive and twice as large for exports as for imports (see Figure 7.6). This is because trade barriers are mostly within the border and levy costs on local firms too, hampering their competitiveness. In addition, service trade barriers reduce competition in the local market, thereby reducing the need for local firms to innovate and explore foreign markets.

The study also estimates that restrictions in sectors such as telecoms result in fewer internet lines and subscribers, with 5 basis points lower STRI resulting in 5 more internet subscribers per 100. For financial services, less restrictive regulations in banking and insurance lead to more developed credit markets. Domestic bank credit relative to GDP is more than twice as high in low STRI countries than with countries with high STRI.

Cristea et al. (2013) calculate the gains from liberalizing trade in the aviation industry. They find that countries that liberalize air transport services gain from expansions in route offerings, reduction in prices, and increase in quantities. If carriers re-orient capacity away from congested routes to routes with little competition, this can yield up to a 31 per cent reduction in prices.

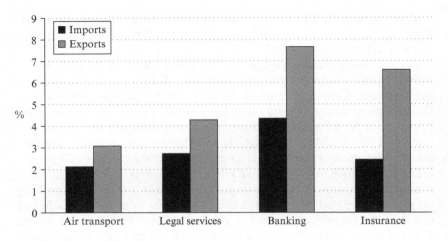

Source: OECD.

Figure 7.6   *Impact of reform on trade in service sector (percentage change
             in exports and imports from 0.05 percentage point's reduction
             in STRI)*

The economic impact of barriers to trade in services is also estimated by
simulating calibrated theoretical models of international trade. The first
step is to construct, on the basis of economic theory, a general or partial
equilibrium model to capture the interaction among different sectors and
agents in the economy. The parameter values are usually chosen from existing estimates. Most studies use the parameter values for the size of service
trade barriers from Hoekman (1995). After the model is calibrated, it is
used to simulate the effects of trade liberalization by comparing the actual
situation with the simulated free trade equilibrium.

The two most commonly used CGE models are various versions of the
Global Trade Analysis Project (GTAP) model and the Michigan Model of
World Production and Trade (MMPT). Studies based on the GTAP models
include: Hertel et al. (2000), the Australian Department of Foreign Affairs
and Trade (1999), Dee and Hanslow (2000), Verikios and Zhang (2004).
Applications of the Michigan model are Brown et al. (1996), Chadha et al.
(2000), and Brown and Stern (2000). OECD (2001a), Dihel (2002) and
Brown and Stern (2000) provide an overview of current work on measuring
and modelling gains from service trade liberalization using CGE modelling.

More recently, François et al. (2008) have computed the possible trade
and welfare effects from liberalization in the EU. The study uses a GTAP
model to estimate the effects of liberalization. They find that gains are

larger if cuts in trade barriers are more comprehensive. In a scenario where full liberalization happens in the service sector, in the long run the UK and the Netherlands will see an increase of 10 per cent in exports of financial services and communication, respectively. The UK has the most service oriented economy in the EU and internal liberalization would benefit it the most. The EU-12 and Austria will see their trade balances in the non-durable sector improve as well. All countries would have positive changes in welfare in the long run.

Global Welfare Gains of Services Liberalization

According to many studies the estimates of benefits from service liberalization vary for individual countries, depending on the initial levels of protection and the assumed reduction in barriers. Studies generally indicate that economies with high initial levels of service trade barriers tend to gain most (in terms of percentage gains to GDP). As these estimated barriers are higher for developing countries than for developed countries, it suggests potentially large benefits for developing countries from liberalization of barriers to trade in services.

In a study by the Centre for International Economics, Sydney and Canberra (2010) the benefits from global trade liberalization in the long run are estimated to range between 0.1 per cent in the US to as high as 2.3 per cent in Thailand. This is assuming liberalization in Mode 1 and 3 of services. The study argues that between 2011 and 2025, the gains from services liberalization can be close to A$5.3 trillion in real GDP and A$3.8 trillion in real consumption.

The EU Commission has estimated the benefits from implementation of the service directive at 0.8 per cent of GDP during the first five years (Monteagudo et al., 2012). For Germany it was estimated that the benefit would be close to 0.45 per cent of GDP and for the UK as high as 1 per cent. In the case that all countries implement the service directive to the same extent as the current EU average it is said that it is possible to have additional growth of 0.4 per cent. In a more optimistic case where all barriers were removed, additional growth would amount to 1.6 per cent.

Hertel et al. (2000) suggest that, while 40 per cent liberalizations in agriculture and manufacturing will each raise global welfare by about US$ 70 billion p.a., a similar liberalization in services could contribute over US$ 300 billion. Dee and Hanslow (1999) and Brown and Stern (1999) were the first CGE studies which explicitly allow for FDI in services. This is crucial given the importance of this mode of supply in international trade in services. Dee and Hanslow (1999, 2000) use the telecom and financial services openness indices to estimate the impact of liberalization of services trade. The study not only allows for entry through FDI, but also distinguishes between entry and operating restrictions. The results indicate that the EU and the US would lose as a result of multilateral service trade liberalization. In large part, this reflects induced changes in the pattern of FDI stocks and an associated loss in rents to the main providers of FDI.

A study by Mattoo et al. (2006) finds that countries with fully open financial and telecom services grow 1.5 percentage points faster than other countries.

Verikios and Zhang (2004) find that complete liberalization of telecommunications and financial services increase world output by 0.2 per cent or US$ 47 billion. According to a study by Brown et al. (2001), world income would increase from the base year of 1995 by 2.5 per cent if all services – not just telecommunications and financial – were liberalized by 33 per cent; and would increase by 7.6 per cent if all barriers were removed (Table 7.5).

A 1999 study published by the European Commission (EC, 1999) comes up with similar results and concludes that trade liberalization – a 20 per cent to 50 per cent global cut in applied protection in agriculture, industrial products and services, plus trade facilitation agreement – would increase annual global welfare by nearly US$ 220 billion to US$ 400 billion. In the first instance, the study looked at across-the-board cuts in trade protection across all agricultural, industrial and services sectors by all countries. Two scenarios were considered: a 20 per cent cut and a 50 per cent global cut in protection. Each of these scenarios was combined with a WTO agreement on trade facilitation, which it is assumed leads to a modest reduction (conservatively estimated at 1 per cent) in the transactions costs associated with

Table 7.5   Global welfare gains from services liberalization (US$ billion)

	Total gain		Services		Goods	
	$ bn	%GDP	$ bn	%GDP	$ bn	%GDP
Brown et al. (2001) projected gains of 33% removal of barriers	613	(2.5)*	390	(1.6)	222	(0.9)
Brown et al. (2001) projected gains of removal of all barriers	1857	(7.6)	1169	(4.8)	689	(2.8)
Dee and Hanslow (2000) projected gains of complete removal of post-Uruguay Round trade barriers	270	(1)	133	(0.5)	133	(0.5)

Note: * Figures in parentheses are the percentage of world real income.

international trade. Their estimates indicate that the potential welfare gain for the EU from the market access plus trade facilitation could amount to an annual windfall of between US$ 46 billion and US$ 92 billion.

The OECD (1997) looked at the effects of a plausible medium-term programme of regulatory reform in eight countries using estimates of efficiency gains in services industries. It reports long-run potential output gains ranging from 3 to 6 per cent in some European countries and Japan to 1 per cent in the US, reflecting the initial state of regulation in different countries.

Welfare Gains to the EU

Here we present a brief summary of those studies that model the EU as a separate economy (see Table 7.6). Most of these studies conclude that the EU will benefit from liberalization in trade in services:

Brown et al. (1996) simulate the impact of a 25 per cent multilateral reduction using Hoekman's (1995) tariff equivalents of service barriers. The estimated welfare gains from the EU are US$ 29 billion (0.4 per cent of GDP) based on assumptions regarding market structure and product differentiation.

Robinson et al. (2002) evaluate the impact of service and non-service sector trade liberalization on the world economy. The EU stands to gain between 0.2 per cent and 4.7 per cent of GDP depending on the underlying assumptions and reform scenarios.

In Chadha et al. (2000), which estimates the impact of a reduction in protection to services trade using Hoekman's (1995) tariff equivalents, the estimated welfare gain for the EU is US$ 66 billion or around 1 per cent of GDP for a 25 per cent reduction in services trade barriers.

Chadha et al. (2000) estimate the gain to the EU and EFTA economies from a 33 per cent reduction in services protection to be US$ 210 billion.

Dee and Hanslow (2000) project the effect of multilateral liberalization of services trade for the EU to be negative, with a loss of $6 billion.

Verikios and Zhang (2004) simulate the impact of elimination of barriers to trade in communication and financial services. They find that a complete liberalization of trade in telecommunications leads to a gain of around US$ 3.5 billion or 0.05 per cent of GDP to the EU. The reforms of the financial services industry result in a similar quantitative gain to the EU.

Brown et al. (2001) study the impact of a reduction in tariffs on agricultural and industrial products and services barriers by 33 per cent (and 100 per cent) in a new WTO trade round. The EU and the EFTA

Table 7.6 Brief summary of CGE studies that model the EU as a separate economy

	Base year	Regions/ sectors	Barriers estimates	Model	Policy simulations	Results (welfare gains to Europe) US$ (% of GDP)
Brown et al. (1996)	1990	8/29	Hoekman (1995)	Michigan	25% multilateral liberalization in services	29 bn (0.4) (0.1 terms of trade change)
Chadha et al. (2000)	1995	7/25	Hoekman (1995)	Michigan	25% multilateral liberalization in services 25% multilateral liberalization in goods and services	66 bn (0.9) 79 bn (1.1)
Chadha et al. (2000)	1995	20/16	Hoekman (1995)	Michigan (with implementation of Uruguay Round in 2005)	33% reduction in bilateral import tariff in services 33% reduction in bilateral import tariff in goods and services	210 bn EU and EFTA 253 bn EU and EFTA
Hertel et al. (2000)	1995	19/22	François & Hoekman (1999); Hoekman (1995)	Modified GTAP (with implementation of Uruguay Round in 2005)	40% cut in agriculture and service protection	

Study	Year		Reference	Model	Scenario	Results
ADFAT (1999)	1995	45/50	Modification of Hoekman (1995)	GTAP framework	50% liberalization in services	73.4 bn (1)
Robinson et al. (2002)	1995	10/11	Brown et al. (1996); Hoekman (1995)	Standard static CGE	50% liberalization in services 50% liberalization in goods and services 50% liberalization in goods and services & transport	(1.2) (1.7) (4.7)
Dee and Hanslow (2000)		18/3	Kalirajan (2000); Warren (2000)	FTAP model with capital mobility and FDI	Multilateral services liberalization Multilateral goods & services liberalization	– 6 bn (0) 0.2 bn (0.1)
Verikios and Zhang (2004)		19/8	Kalirajan (2000); Warren (2000)	FTAP model with capital mobility and FDI	In post Uruguay Round environment, elimination of barriers to trade in communication Elimination of barriers to trade in financial services	3.5 bn (0.5) 3.4 bn (0.5)

stand to gain US$ 169 billion (and US$ 507 billion), which is 28 per cent of the global welfare gains.

Due to different databases on services trade as well as different assumptions about liberalization policies, the estimates from different studies are not strictly comparable. However, the results indicate that the welfare gains from liberalization of trade in services would be substantial for EU member countries as well as for the global economy.

Given the high share of services in EU GDP, it is hardly surprising that the simulations suggest that the EU stands to make large gains in the service sector. The prediction of potentially large welfare gains for the EU derives mainly from its current high level of protection. Liberalization of the services sector will provide the incentive for resources to move out of relatively highly protected sectors and into sectors in which the EU has a comparative advantage or which benefit from scale economies. With further liberalization, the EU services sector would be in a relatively stronger position to expand and take advantage of improved access to foreign markets.

Messerlin (2001) uses partial equilibrium analysis to assess the cost to EU consumers from protection in three service sectors (films, passenger air transport and telecommunications) and estimates the cost of protection as 16 per cent of their value added (Table 7.7).

Dobson and Jacquet (1998) evaluate the impact of the Financial Services Agreement (FSA) at the WTO in December 1997. The present value of total benefits from financial services reform by 2010 would be, with an assumed discount rate of 12 per cent, US$ 1 trillion. The EU would benefit in the region of 0.7 per cent of GDP. This simple calculation shows that financial reform holds significant promise. Empirical studies in Europe and the US

Table 7.7   Estimated welfare effects of liberalizing selected services in the EU

	Ad valorem tariff equiv.	Induced increase in imports (€ billion)	Consumer surplus gain (€ billion)		Net welfare gain (€ billion)
			A	B	B
Films (France)	76.8	0.3	0.6	0.4	0.3
Air transport	71.0	2.3	9.0	8.8	7.0
Telecom	45.2	5.7	5.9	4.0	2.8

Notes: A: based on François and Hall (1997) model; B: based on Hufbauer and Elliott (1994) model.

Source: Messerlin (2001).

of efficiency differences among banks indicate the following: banks could reduce their costs and increase profits by between 20 and 50 per cent by increasing productive efficiency; thrifts and credit unions could achieve 20 per cent efficiency gains by improving managerial efficiency and by using the same sophisticated technology as is used by best-practice institutions; national bank regulatory agencies could make efficiency gains of a similar magnitude by achieving greater economies of scale in clearing and payments services; and insurers (where comparable data are scarce) are estimated to be between 45 and 90 per cent efficient (Berger et al., 1993). In telecommunications it is estimated that the liberalization would cut the cost of international calls by more than 80 per cent and the Institute of International Economics calculated that it could cut telecom bills by up to US$1 trillion, equivalent to 4 per cent of world GDP (Artis and Nixson, 2001). Mr Ian Taylor, the former UK Science and Technology Minister, has been quoted as saying 'the market [telecom] is already worth $600bn annually and growing at 10 per cent a year. Some analysts predicted an extra £20bn worth of telecom business for the UK alone over the next 10 to 15 years' (Williams and Cane, 1997).

Not much work has been undertaken to evaluate the effects of liberalization of service trade via mode 4 – temporary movement of natural persons (TMNP). Although TMNP currently accounts for only 1.4 per cent of the value of services trade (Karsenty, 2000) (this low figure arises from the very high barriers to TMNP), this mode of service delivery possibly offers the greatest potential returns to liberalization. Based on the global applied general equilibrium model of South–North temporary movement of labour, Winters (2002) suggests that an increase in developed countries' quotas on the inward movements of both skilled and unskilled temporary workers equivalent to 3 per cent of their workforces would generate an estimated increase in world welfare of over US$ 150 billion p.a.. These gains are shared between developing and developed countries and owe more to unskilled than to skilled labour mobility.

From the above discussion it is clear that estimates of economic impact on the EU vary widely. At one extreme, Dee and Hanslow (1999, 2000) predict that the EU is likely to lose rather than gain from trade liberalization in services. At the other extreme, Brown et al. (2001) show that the EU is expected to gain as much as 2.5 per cent of GDP. The magnitude of welfare effects is strongly dependent on the accuracy of estimates of services barriers and on the various modelling assumptions. The estimates of different services barriers vary on the basis of the data sources and estimation techniques employed. The studies which use Hoekman's estimates for the initial interventions generally report large welfare gains from services trade liberalization. By contrast, studies which employ the estimates determined on the basis of price or quantity impact measures tend to generate lower, though still sizeable welfare gains. Even though the quality of esti-mates of barriers has been improving both in terms of coverage and the range of barriers addressed, it is difficult to determine if these estimates are realistic as a number of limitations remain, related mainly to data avail-ability and the nature of barriers. Major shortcomings are also associated with the weight-assignment for different categories of restrictions.

7.6   CONCLUSIONS

What all this shows is that services liberalization, with its possibilities for welfare enhancement, is at best a work in progress and at worst a triumph of hope over experience of vested interest opposition. At this point EU liberalization is extremely limited and has focused more on harmonizing regulation than on introducing competition. In this book we assume that services remain essentially protected within the EU by persistent national measures and that the UK already enjoys a liberal services regime and sells its services around the world at world prices.

NOTES

1. Non-market services comprise branches covering general public services, non-market services of education and research provided by general government and private non-profit institutions, non-market services of health provided by general government and private non-profit institutions, domestic services and other non-market services. The OECD describes non-market services as those services that are provided as wholly free of charge or at a fee which is 50 per cent below the production costs.
2. A statistical domain known as Foreign Affiliates Trade in Services (FATS) is being devel-oped by the UN Statistical Commission to measure international trade in services via mode 3. It would measure sales of services by affiliates established in foreign countries to local persons and so correspond to the GATS notion of service trade through commercial presence.
3. The seat tax is a non-discriminatory excise tax imposed on both foreign and French films. An indirect tax of roughly 11 per cent is levied on every seat sold in French cinemas, independent of the nationality of the film shown. It is also one of the sources of subsidies which are granted to French movie producers and cinema owners. As a result, in practice, the seat tax is considered discriminatory.

Bibliography

AC Nielsen Survey (2000), 'A report into international price comparisons', prepared for the Department of Trade and Industry, UK, 13 February.

Agriculture & Horticulture Development Board (2013), 'The impact of CAP reform on direct payments to farms in the UK and other member states', special report.

Anderson, K. (2010), 'Agricultural price and trade policy reform in developing countries since 1960', World Bank Research Working Paper, WP5165, Washington, DC: World Bank.

Aristotelous, K. (2001), 'Exchange-rate volatility, exchange-rate regime, and trade volume: evidence from the UK–US export function (1889–1999)', *Economics Letters*, 72, 87–94.

Arthur Andersen (1999), 'Study for Dixons', Press Release, 19 July, available at: www.dixons.com, reported in J. Haskel and H. Wolf (2000), 'From Big Macs to iMacs: what do international price comparisons tell us?', *World Economics*, April–June, 1(2), 167–78.

Artis, M.J and N. Nixson (2001), *The Economics of the European Union*, 3rd edn, Oxford: Oxford University Press.

Australian Department of Foreign Affairs and Trade (DFAT) (1999), *Global Trade Reform: Maintaining Momentum*, Canberra: AusInfo.

Bacchetta, P. and E. van Winkoop (2000), 'Does exchange-rate stability increase trade and welfare?', *American Economic Review*, December, 90(5), 1093–109.

Bailey, M., G.S. Tavlas and M. Ulan (1987), 'The impact of exchange rate volatility on export growth: some theoretical considerations and empirical results', *Journal of Policy Modelling*, 9, 225–43.

Barrell, R. (2002), 'The UK and EMU: choosing the regime', *National Institute Economic Review*, April, 180, 54–71.

Barrell, R. and K. Dury (2000), 'Choosing the regime: macroeconomic effects of UK entry into EU', *Journal of Common Market Studies*, November, 38(4), 625–44.

Beecroft, A. (2012), 'Report on employment law', known as The Beecroft Report, London: Department of Business Innovation and Skills, May, available as publication Ref. 12/825 at www.gov.uk/government/publications/employment-law-review-report-beecroft.

Berger, N., W.C. Hunter and S.G. Timme (1993), 'The efficiency of financial institutions: a review and preview of research past, present and future', *Journal of Banking & Finance*, 17(2–3), 221–49.

BIS (2010a), 'UK trade performance: patterns in UK and global trade growth', BIS Economics Paper No. 8, London: Department for Business Innovation and Skills.

BIS (2010b), 'Manufacturing in the UK: an economic analysis of the sector', BIS Economics Paper No. 10A, London: Department for Business Innovation and Skills.

Blonigen, B.A. and T.J. Prusa (2001), 'Anti-dumping', NBER Working Paper No. w8398, July.

Blonigen, B.A. and T.J. Prusa (2003), 'The cost of antidumping: the devil is in the details', *Journal of Policy Reform*, 6(4), 233–46.

Borchert, I., B. Gootiiz and A. Mattoo (2012), 'Policy barriers to international trade in services: evidence from a new database', World Bank Policy Research Working Paper No. 6109, Washington, DC: World Bank.

Borrell, B. and L.J. Hubbart (2000), 'Global economic effects of the EU Common Agricultural Policy', *Economic Affairs: Reforming the CAP*, 20(2), 18–26.

Bouët, A. and D. Laborde (2009), 'The potential cost of a failed Doha Round', Issue Brief No. 56, Washington, DC: International Food Policy Research Institute.

Boylaud, O. and G. Nicoletti (2001), 'Regulation, market structure and performance in telecommunications', *OECD Economic Studies*, 2001(1), 99–142.

Bradford, S.C. (2000), 'Paying the price: the welfare effects of trade barriers and inflated distribution margins in OECD countries', May, Brigham Young University.

Bradford, S.C. (2003), 'Paying the price: final goods protection in OECD countries', *Review of Economics and Statistics*, 85(1), 24–37.

Bradford, S.C. and R.Z. Lawrence (2004), *Has Globalization Gone Far Enough? The Costs of Fragmented Markets*, Washington, DC: Institute for International Economics.

Britain in Europe (2000), *The Case for the Euro*, Richard Layard, Willem Buiter, David Currie, Christopher Huhne, Will Hutton, Peter Kenen, Robert Mundell and Adair Turner (authors), London: Britain in Europe.

Brown, D.K. and R.M. Stern (1999), 'Measurement and modelling of the economic effects of trade and investment barriers in services', paper prepared for the Coalition of Services Industries (CSI) World Services Congress, Atlanta, GA, 1–3 November.

Brown, D.K. and R.M. Stern (2000), 'Measurement and modeling of the economic effects of trade and investment barriers in services', School of Public Policy Discussion Paper No. 453, University of Michigan.

Brown, D.K., A.V. Deardorff and R.M. Stern (1996), 'Modeling multilateral liberalization in services', *Asia-Pacific Economic Review*, 2, 21–34.

Brown, D.K., A.V. Deardorff and R.M. Stern (2001), 'Impacts on NAFTA members of multilateral and regional trading arrangements and initiatives and harmonization of NAFTA's external tariffs', Discussion Paper No. 471, Ann Arbor, MI: University of Michigan.

Brown, D.K., A.V. Deardorff and R.M. Stern (2002), 'CGE modeling and analysis of multilateral and regional negotiating options', in R.M. Stern (ed.), *Issues and Options for US–Japan Trade Policies*, Ann Arbor, MI: University of Michigan Press, pp. 23–76.

Bungay, F. (2012), 'EU agricultural protection: tariffs and the CAP', London: Trade Policy Research Centre.

Bush, J. (ed.) (2001), 'The economic case against the euro', New Europe for the No Campaign, available at: www.no-euro.com.

Centre for International Economics (2010), 'Quantifying the benefits of services trade liberalisation', paper prepared for Department of Foreign Affairs and Trade, June.

Chadha, R. (2001), 'GATS and the developing countries: a case study of India', in Robert M. Stern (ed.), *Services in the International Economy: Measurement and Modeling, Sectoral and Country Studies, and Issues in the WTO Services Negotiations*, Ann Arbor, MI: University of Michigan Press, pp. 245–66.

Chadha, R., D. Brown, A. Deardorff and R. Stern (2000), 'Computational analysis of the impact on India of the Uruguay Round and the forthcoming WTO trade negotiations', School of Public Policy Discussion Paper No. 459, Ann Arbor, MI: University of Michigan.

Clark, Ximena, David Dollar and Alejandro Micco (2004), 'Port efficiency, maritime transport costs, and bilateral trade', *Journal of Development Economics*, 75(2), 417–50.

Colecchia, A. (2001), 'The impact of information and communications technologies on output growth: issues and preliminary findings', OECD STI Working Paper No. 11, Geneva.

Congdon, T. (2014a), 'How much does the European Union cost Britain?', London: UK Independence Party.

Congdon, T. (2014b), 'The City of London in retreat: the EU's attack on Britain's most successful industry', London: The Bruges Group.

Constantinescu, C., A. Mattoo and M. Ruta (2015), 'The global trade slowdown: cyclical or structural?', IMF Working Paper No. WP/15/6,

Washington, DC: World Bank Group, Development Research Group, Trade and International Integration Team.

Corugedo, E. and E.R. Ruiz (2014), 'The EU Services Directive: gains from further liberalisation', IMF Working Paper No. WP/14/113, Washington, DC: European Department.

Costinot, A. and A. Rodriguez-Clare (2013), 'Trade theory with numbers: quantifying the consequences of globalization', CEPR Discussion Paper No. 9398, March, London: Centre for Economic and Policy Research.

Cristea, A., D. Hummels, L. Puzzello and M. Avetisyan (2013), 'Trade and the greenhouse gas emissions from international freight transport', *Journal of Environmental Economics and Management*, 65(1), 153–73.

Danish Research Institute of Food Economics (2013), website available at: www.foi.dk.

Decreux, Y. and L. Fontagné (2011), 'Economic impact of potential outcome of the DDA II', CEPII–CIREM, European Commission DG Trade.

Dee, P. (2005), 'The Australia–US Free Trade Agreement: an assessment', Asia Pacific Economic Papers No. 345, Australia–Japan Research Centre, Crawford School of Public Policy, The Australian National University.

Dee, P. and K. Hanslow (1999), 'Modelling liberalisation of services', paper presented at Productivity Commission and Australian National University Joint Conference, Australian National University, Canberra, 26–27 June.

Dee, P. and K. Hanslow (2000), 'Multilateral liberalisation of services trade', Productivity Commission Staff Research Paper, Canberra: AusInfo.

DEFRA (2013), 'Implementation of CAP reform in England: evidence paper', London: Department for Environment Food & Rural Affairs.

Dihel, N. (2002), 'Measuring the benefits of services trade liberalisation', background paper, OECD–World Bank Services Experts Meeting, OECD, Paris, 4–5 March.

Dimaranan, B., T. Hertel and R. Keeney (2003), 'OECD domestic support and developing countries', World Institute for Development Economics Research (WIDER) Discussion Paper No. 2003/32, New York: WIDER.

Dobson, W. and P. Jacquet (1998), *Financial Services Liberalization in the WTO*, Washington, DC: Institute for International Economics.

Doove, S., O. Gabbitas, D. Nguyen-Hong and J. Owen (2001), 'Price effects of regulation: telecommunications, air passenger transport and electricity supply', Productivity Commission Staff Research Paper, AusInfo, Canberra, October.

EC (European Commission) (1990), 'One market, one money: an

evaluation of the potential benefits and costs of forming an economic and monetary union', *European Economy*, 44, October.

EC (European Commission) (1999), 'The Millennium Round: an economic appraisal', European Commission Directorate General for Economic and Financial Affairs, Economic Paper No. 139, Brussels: European Commission.

EC (European Commission) (2010), 'An integrated industrial policy for the globalisation era: putting competitiveness and sustainability at centre stage', Brussels: European Commission.

EC (European Commission) (2012), 'The Common Agricultural Policy', Luxembourg: Publications Office of the European Union.

EC (European Commission) (2013a), 'Overview of CAP reform 2014–2020', Agricultural Policy Perspective Brief, No. 5, Brussels: European Commission.

EC (European Commission) (2013b), 'Trade, growth and jobs', contribution from the Commission to the February 2013 European Council Debate on Trade, Growth and Jobs, Brussels: European Commission.

EC (European Commission) (2013c), 'Competing in global value chains: EU industrial structure report', Brussels: European Commission.

EC (European Commission) (2013d), 'Fitness Check – Internal Aviation Market Report on the suitability of economic regulation of the European air transport market and of selected ancillary services', Commission Staff working document, Brussels: European Commission.

EC (European Commission) (2014a), 'Advancing manufacturing – advancing Europe' report of the Task Force on Advanced Manufacturing for Clean Production, European Commission Staff Working Document, Brussels: European Commission.

EC (European Commission) (2014b), 'More transparent and safer financial markets', EC statement/14/129, Brussels: European Commission.

EU (European Union) (2000), 'Impact of Agenda 2000 decisions for CAP reform on consumers', in 'Impact analyses of the Agenda 2000 decisions for CAP reform', Directorate-General for Agriculture of the European Commission, Brussels, February, pp. 85–90.

EU (European Union) (2011), 'Textile and clothing sector and EU trade policy', February, Brussels.

Eurostat (2014), 'Statistics explained: professional, scientific and technical activity statistics – NACE Rev. 2', November.

Fernández Corugedo, E. and E. Pérez Ruiz (2014), 'The EU services directive: gains from further liberalization', IMF Working Paper No. 14/113, Washington, DC: IMF.

Fillat-Castejon, C., J.F. François and J.M. Woerz (2008), 'Cross-border trade and FDI in services', Economics Working Papers No. 2008-12, Department of Economics, Johannes Kepler University Linz, Austria.

Findlay, C. and T. Warren (eds) (2000), *Impediments to Trade in Services: Measurement and Policy Implications*, London and New York: Routledge.

Flandreau, M. (2001), 'The bank, the states and the market: an Austro-Hungarian tale for Euroland, 1867–1914', Oesterreichische Nationalbank Working Paper No. 43, Vienna: Oesterreichische Nationalbank.

Fontagné, L. and Y. Decreux (2013), 'What did happen in the DDA? Quantifying the role of negotiation modalities', CEPII Working Paper No. 2013-38.

Fontagné, L., A. Guillin and C. Mitaritonna (2011), 'Estimations of tariff equivalents for the service sector', CEPII Working Paper No. 2011-24.

Fontagné, L., T. Mayer and G. Ottaviano (2009), 'Of markets, products and prices: the effects of the euro on European firms', *Intereconomics: Review of European Economic Policy*, 44(3), 149–58.

François, J.F. (1999), 'A gravity approach to measuring services protection', mimeo, Erasmus University, Rotterdam.

François, J.F. and H. Glismann (2000), 'The cost of EU trade protection in textiles and clothing', Kiel Institute of World Economics Working Paper No. 997, Kiel.

François, J.F. and H.K. Hall (1997), 'Partial equilibrium modelling', in J.F. François and K.A. Reinert (eds), *Applied Methods for Trade Policy Analysis: A Handbook*, Cambridge: Cambridge University Press.

François, J.F. and B. Hoekman (1999), 'Market access in the services sectors', mimeo, Tinbergen Institute.

François, J.F., B. MacDonald and H. Nordström (1995), 'Assessing the Uruguay Round', in W. Martin and A. Winters (eds), *The Uruguay Round and the Developing Economies*, World Bank Discussion Paper 201, Washington, DC: World Bank.

François, J., O. Pindyuk and J. Woerz (2008), 'Trade effects of services trade liberalization in the EU', IIDE Discussion Paper No. 20080801, Institute for International and Development Economics.

François, J., O. Pindyuk and J. Woerz (2009), 'International transactions in services: data on international trade and FDI in the service sectors', University of Linz, Discussion Paper No. 20090802, Institute for International and Development Economics.

François, J., H. Van Mejil and F. Van Tongeren (2003), 'Trade liberalization and developing countries under the Doha Round', Discussion Paper No. 4032, London: Centre For Economic Policy Research.

Gabaix, X. (2011), 'The granular origins of aggregate fluctuations', *Econometrica*, 79, 733–72.

Gönenç, R. and G. Nicoletti (2000), 'Regulation, market structure and performance in air passenger transportation', OECD Economics Department Working Papers No. 254, Paris: OECD.

Government Office for Science (2013), 'Future of manufacturing: a new era of opportunity and challenge for the UK', London: The Government Office for Science.

Guillin, A. (2011), 'Assessment of tariff equivalents for services considering the zero-flows', unpublished working paper.

Gulbrandsen, O. and A. Lindbeck (1973), *The Economics of the Agricultural Sector*, Stockholm: O. Industriens Utredningsinstitut (Swedish edn, 1969).

Gwartney, J., R. Lawson and J. Hall (eds) (2012), *Economic Freedom of the World: 2012 Annual Report*, Vancouver: Fraser Institute.

Hertel, T.W. (ed.) (1997), *Global Trade Analysis: Modelling and Applications*, Cambridge: Cambridge University Press.

Hertel, T.W. (2000), 'Potential gains from reducing trade barriers in manufacturing, services and agriculture', *Federal Reserve Bank of St Louis Review*, 82(4), 77–99.

Hertel, T.W., K. Anderson, J.F. François and W. Martin (2000), 'Agriculture and non-agricultural liberalization in the Millennium Round', Policy Discussion Paper No. 0016, Centre for International Economic Studies, University of Adelaide.

Hoekman, B. (1995), 'Assessing the General Agreement on Trade in Services', in W. Martin and L.A. Winters (eds), *The Uruguay Round and the Developing Economies*, Washington, DC: World Bank, pp. 327–64.

Hoekman, B. (2006), 'Liberalizing trade in services: a survey', World Bank and CEPR, Research Working Paper No. 4030, Washington, DC: World Bank.

Hoekman, B. and P. Braga (1997), 'Protection and trade in services: a survey', *Open Economies Review*, 8, 285–308.

House of Commons (2000), 'What would the euro cost British business?', Trade and Industry Committee Report, Cmnd. HC755.

Howarth, C., A. Kullmann and P. Swidlicki (2012), 'More for less: making the EU's farm policy work for growth and the environment', Open Europe.

Hufbauer, G.C. and K.A. Elliott (1994), *Measuring the Costs of Protection in the United States*, Washington, DC: Institute of International Economics.

Hulten, Charles R. (1978), 'Growth accounting with intermediate inputs', *The Review of Economic Studies*, 45(3), 511–18.

IMF (2002), 'United States: selected issues', IMF country report No. 07/265, August, Washington, DC: IMF.

IMF (2014), 'Legacies, clouds, uncertainties', World Economic and Financial Surveys, Washington, DC: IMF.

Johnson, D.G. (1995), *Less than Meets the Eye: The Modest Impact of CAP Reform*, London: Centre for Policy Studies.

Jones, Charles I. (2011), 'Intermediate goods and weak links in the theory of economic development', *American Economic Journal: Macroeconomics*, 3(2), 1–28.

Kaleeswaran, K., G. McGuire, D. Nguyen-Hong and M. Schuele (2000), 'The price impact of restrictions on banking services', in C. Findlay and T. Warren (eds), *Impediments to Trade in Services: Measurement and Policy Implications*, London: Routledge, pp. 215–30.

Kalirajan, K. (2000), 'Restrictions on trade in distribution services', Productivity Commission Staff Research Paper, AusInfo, Canberra.

Kalirajan, K., G. McGuire, D. Nguyen-Hong and M. Schuele (2001), 'The price impact of restrictions on banking services', in C. Findlay and T. Warren (eds), *Impediments to Trade in Services: Measurement and Policy Implications*, New York: Routledge, pp. 215–30.

Karsenty, G. (2000), 'Assessing trade in services by mode of supply', in P. Sauvé and R. Stern (eds), *GATS 2000: New Directions in Services Trade Liberalisation*, Washington, DC: Brookings Institution, pp. 33–56.

Kee, H.L., A. Nicita and M. Olarreaga (2009), 'Estimating trade restrictiveness indices', *Economic Journal*, 119, 172–99.

Keijzer, N. and M. King (2012), 'Monitoring the effects of the Common Agricultural Policy in developing countries: a review of the institutional options', London: Overseas Development Institute.

Kerkela, L., H. Lehtonen and J. Niemi (2005), 'The impacts of WTO export subsidy abolition on the agri-food industry in the EU: a preliminary assessment', VATT Discussion Papers No. 355, Helsinki: Government Institute for Economic Research.

Leach, G. (2001), *The Third EMU Test*, London: Business for Sterling.

Love, P. and R. Lattimore (2009), 'Protectionism? Tariffs and other barriers to trade', in *International Trade: Free, Fair and Open?*, Paris: OECD Publishing.

Mattoo, A., R. Rathindran and A. Subramanian (2006), 'Measuring services trade liberalisation and its impact on economic growth: an illustration', *Journal of Economic Integration*, March, 21(1), 64–98.

McCallum, J. (1995), 'National borders matter: Canada–US regional trade patterns', *American Economic Review*, June, 85, 615–23.

McGuire, G. and Schuele, M. (2000), 'Restrictiveness of international trade in banking services', in C. Findlay and T. Warren (eds), *Impediments to Trade in Services: Measurement and Policy Implications*, London and New York: Routledge, pp. 201–14.

Messerlin, P.A. (1990), 'Anti-dumping regulations or pro-cartel law? The EC chemical cases', *The World Economy*, December, 13(4), 465–92.

Messerlin, P.A. (2001), *Measuring the Costs of Protection in Europe: European Commercial Policy in the 2000s*, Washington, DC: Institute of International Economics.

Minford, L. (2015), 'The impact of policy on UK output and productivity growth, 1970–2009: testing an open economy DSGE model', PhD thesis, Cardiff University.

Minford, P. (1998), *Markets not Stakes: the Triumph of Capitalism and the Stakeholder Fallacy*, London: Orion Business Books.

Minford, P. (2001), 'Tests 1 and 2: flexibility and the costs in economic variability', in J. Bush (ed.), *The Economic Case against the Euro*, New Europe for the No Campaign, available at: www.no-euro.com, pp. 67–78.

Minford, P. (2002), 'Should Britain join the Euro?', London: The Institute of Economic Affairs.

Minford, P. and D. Peel (2002), *Advanced Macroeconomics: a Primer*, Cheltenham, UK and Northampton, MA, USA: Edward Elgar Publishing.

Minford, P., E. Nowell and J. Riley (1997), 'Trade, technology and labour markets in the world economy, 1970–90: a computable general equilibrium analysis', *The Journal of Development Studies*, December, 34(2), 1–34.

Monopolies and Mergers Commission (1992), 'New motor cars: a report on the supply of new motor cars within the UK', 2 vols, cmnd. 1808, London: HMSO.

Monteagudo, J., A. Rutkowski and D. Lorenzani (2012), 'The economic impact of the service directive: a first assessment following implementation', Economic Papers No. 456, European Commission,.

Nguyen-Hong, D. (2000), 'Restrictions on trade in professional services', Productivity Commission Staff Research Paper, August, Canberra: AusInfo.

Nicoletti, G. and S. Scarpetta (2001), 'Interactions between product and labour market regulations: do they affect employment? Evidence from OECD Countries', paper presented at the Banco de Portugal Conference on 'Labour Market Institutions and Economic Outcomes', Cascais, 3–4 June.

Niemietz, K. (2013), 'Redefining the poverty debate', London: The Institute of Economic Affairs.

Nitsch, V. (2001), 'Honey I just shrunk the Currency Union effect on trade', mimeo, Bankgesellschaft Berlin.

OECD (1997), 'Assessing barriers to trade in services: a pilot study on accountancy services', TD/TC/WP(97)26, Working Party of the Trade Committee, Paris: OECD.

OECD (2000), 'Quantification of the costs to national welfare of barriers to trade in services: a scoping paper', TD/TC/WP(2000)32, Working Party of the Trade Committee, 4–5 December, Paris: OECD.

OECD (2001a), 'Open services markets matter', TD/TC/WP(2001)24/ PART1/REV1, Working Party of the Trade Committee, Trade Directorate.

OECD (2001b), 'Towards more liberal agricultural trade: Policy Brief', OECD Observer, November, Paris.

OECD (2014a), 'Services Trade Restrictiveness Index (STRI): Policy Brief', Paris: OECD.

OECD (2014b), 'Agricultural Policy Monitoring and Evaluation, 2014', Paris: OECD.

OECD (2014c), 'The WTO Trade Facilitation Agreement: potential impact on trade costs', Trade and Agriculture Directorate, Paris: OECD.

OECD–WTO (2013), OCED–WTO Database on Trade in Value-Added (TiVA).

OECD, WTO and World Bank Group (2014), 'Global Value Chains: challenges, opportunities, and implications for policy', report prepared for submission to the G20 Trade Ministers Meeting, Sydney, Australia.

Ottaviano, G., J.P. Pessoa, T. Sampson and J. Van Reenen (2014), 'The costs and benefits of leaving the EU', London School of Economics, Centre for Economic Performance, 13 May.

Patton, M., S. Feng, J. Davis and J. Binfield (2013), 'Impact of CAP post-2013 reforms on agriculture in the UK', Agricultural and Food Economics, FAPRI-UK project report.

Persson, T. (2001), 'Currency unions and trade: how large is the treatment effect?', *Economic Policy*, 33, 433–48.

Robinson, S., Z. Wang and W. Martin (2002), 'Capturing the implications of services trade liberalization', *Economic Systems Research*, 14(1), 3–33.

Roland-Holst, D.W., K.A. Reinert and C.R. Shiells (1994), 'A general equilibrium analysis of North American integration', in J.F. François and C.R. Shiells (eds), *Modelling Trade Policy: AGE Models of North American Free Trade*, Cambridge: Cambridge University Press.

Rose, A.K. (1999), 'One money, one market: estimating the effect of common currencies on trade', CEPR Discussion Paper No. 2329, December, London: Centre for Economic Policy Research. A version appeared in *Economic Policy*, 2000 (April), 30, 7–45, with comments by economists on the Economic Policy Panel.

Roseveare, D., W. Leibfritz, D. Fore and E. Wurzel (1996), 'Ageing populations, pension systems and government budgets: simulations for

20 OECD countries', OECD Economics Department Working Paper No. 168, Paris: OECD.

Rotherham, L. (2010), 'Food for thought: how the Common Agricultural Policy costs families nearly £400 a year', London: The Taxpayers' Alliance and Global Vision.

Stern, Robert M. and Alan V. Deardorff (2006), 'Globalization's bystanders: does trade liberalization hurt countries that do not participate?', *World Development*, 34(8), 1419–29.

Stoeckel, A. (2002), 'Opportunities of a century to liberalise farm trade', Canberra: Rural Industries Research and Development Corporation.

Stoeckel, A.B. and J. Breckling (1989), 'Some economy wide effects of agricultural policies in the European Community: a general equilibrium study', in A.B. Stoeckel, D. Vincent and S. Cuthbertson (eds), *Macroeconomic Consequences of Farm Support Policies*, Durham, NC: Duke University Press.

Stollinger, R. (2009), 'Global patterns of trade specialisation and club convergence: past and current patterns of trade specialization', Challenges for Europe in the world in 2025, European Commission within the Seventh Framework Programme.

Stollinger, R., N. Foster-McGregor, M. Holzner, M. Landesmann, J. Poschl and R. Stehrer (2013), 'A "manufacturing imperative" in the EU: Europe's position in global manufacturing and the role of industrial policy', Research Reports No. 391, The Vienna Institute for International Economic Studies (WIIW).

Sunday Times (1998), Sunday Times survey, August 1998, as reported in Jonathan Haskel and Holger Wolf (2000), 'From Big Macs to iMacs: what do international price comparisons tell us?', *World Economics*, 1(2), 167–78.

Thom, R. and B. Walsh (2002), 'The effect of a currency union on trade: lessons from the Irish experience', forthcoming in *European Economic Review*, available at http://www.ucd.ie/~economic/staff/bwalsh/bwalsh.html.

United Nations (2014), 'Trade and development report 2014', Geneva: United Nations Conference on Trade and Development (UNCTAD).

United Nations Statistics Division (2008), 'International trade in services and tourism', available at: http://unstats.un.org/unsd/tradeserv/brochure%20SITSS%202010.pdf.

Verikios, G. and X. Zhang (2004), 'The economic effects of removing barriers to trade in telecommunications', *The World Economy*, 27(3), 435–58.

Veugelers, E. (ed.) (2013), *Manufacturing Europe's Future*, Brussels: Bruegel Blueprint Series.

Walsh, K. (2006), 'Trade in services: does gravity hold? A gravity model approach to estimating barriers to service trade', Discussion Paper Series No. 183, IIIS, Revenue Commissioners.

Warren, T. (2000), 'Identification of impediments to trade and investment in telecommunications services', in C. Findlay and T. Warren (eds), *Impediments to Trade in Services: Measurement and Policy Implications*, London: Routledge, pp. 71–84.

Warren, T. and C. Findlay (2000), 'How significant are the barriers? Measuring impediments to trade in services', in Pierre Sauve and Robert M. Stern (eds), *GATS 2000: New Directions in Services Trade Liberalization*, Washington, DC: Brookings Institution.

Williams, F. and A. Cane (1997), 'World Telecoms pact to slash cost of calls', *Financial Times*, 17 February.

Winters, L.A. (2002), 'The economic implications of liberalising Mode 4 trade', paper prepared for the Joint WTO–World Bank Symposium on 'The Movement of Natural Persons (Mode 4) Under the GATS', WTO, Geneva, 11–12 April.

WTO (World Trade Organization) (2013), 'Trade Policy Review', Trade Policy Review Body, WT/TPR/S/284.

WTO (World Trade Organization) (2014), 'Service profiles 2014', Geneva: World Trade Organization.

WTO, ITC, UNCTAD (2013), 'World tariff profiles 2013', Geneva: World Trade Organization.

WTO, ITC, UNCTAD (2014), 'World tariff profiles 2014', Geneva: World Trade Organization.

Zahrnt, V. (2011), 'Food security and the EU's common agricultural policy: facts against fears', ECIPE Working Paper No. 01/2011.

Index